Shahriar

Shahriar

شهریار

Phoenix of the desert: reborn out of darkness

Bahram and Shahin Bekhradnia

Dedicated to the memory of our mother Laal, without whose love and support Shahriar would not have been able to live the life he did, and to their grandchildren who gave them so much joy.

ISBN: 978-1-0369-1357-1

Contents

Preface

This book tells the story of Shahriar, our father, born into a Zoroastrian peasant family in a village in the deserts of Iran, and of his rising against the odds to become an officer in the Imperial Iranian Army of Shah Reza Pahlavi; of the tragic injury which left him blind; of how, following an undertaking given by the Shah, he came to England for (unsuccessful) treatment and stayed here, raising two children with his remarkable and devoted wife Laal; of how he railed against the Islamic revolution; and of how he finally died, after an extraordinary life, aged 87, in Oxford England, just 6 weeks after Laal.

In one generation and despite his disability, he raised himself from a hopeless and peasant background and brought up his two children in their different ways to become successful members of the English middle classes.

In telling his story we have relied a great deal on what might be termed oral history – our memories of conversations with him and with our mother about the past and with others who were contemporaries. We have also been able to draw upon the many interviews conducted in the course of Shahin's 1995 thesis on "Identity and Change among Iranian Zoroastrians in the 20th Century"

With regard to his life in Iran, there are no documents, but there are a few photographs which we have been able to reproduce. Inevitably, because many of these are somewhat old and were taken on unsophisticated cameras, their quality is not as good as we would have liked, but they at least impart a flavour of what is intended.

In describing his time in England and our family life, we have been able to rely on our personal memories, but also on extensive documentation held in the St Dunstan's and Moorfields Eye Hospital archives, as well as a mass of letters and other documents which our mother, for reasons best known to herself but for which we are grateful, held on to.

Every significant incident described in this book occurred as described. In some cases we have embellished the incident with what we have been told about the emotions and feelings that surrounded it. In a very small number we have exercised a degree of poetic licence in expanding what we know about Shahriar's thoughts and emotions. But in its entirety, and to the very best of our ability, this is an accurate account of his life, based on fact. It tells a remarkable story.

Bahram and Shahin Bekhradnia
Oxfordshire, January 2025

Acknowledgements

We are indebted to many people who informed, encouraged and critiqued this book as it was developed. Among them – and there will be others not mentioned to whom we apologise – are the following:

Mark Wheeler of St Dunstan's, who kindly himself inspected the archives for information about Shahriar, and later opened the archives to us.

Destre, the very helpful archivist of Moorfields Eye Hospital, who opened the hospital archives to us and enabled us to locate the relevant medical records that are related to Shahriar.

Guy Mole, a consultant ophthalmologist in Oxford, who enabled us to decipher and interpret the otherwise indecipherable handwriting, abbreviations and notes in the hospital records.

Angela Coulter who provided valuable advice at the outset.

Our good friends Stephen Eeley and John Marzillier who offered valuable criticisms and suggestions on the draft.

Akbar Ghalamsiah, the author of a book about Jafarabad and its inhabitants.

Dr James Younessi in Australia, who advised about the medals and decorations.

Fellow military veteran Zartosht Setudeh, now living in London who was able to provide invaluable information about Shahriar's time in the Military Academy and army.

Mehraban Javanmardian, the headman of Jafarabad who answered our many questions and provided photographs.

Shirin Dave, daughter of Shahriar's cousin Sarvar, now living in Kent who provided valuable insights into Shahriar's time in Bombay.

Iran, with significant places mentioned in text highlighted

PART 1: IRAN

Childhood

Shahriar did not know the date of his birth – he did not even know the month, and we variously celebrated his birthday on 4 January and 2 August. But he was pretty sure that the year was 1916, so that has been our assumption.

He was born to Shirin and Khorsand – no surnames at that time[1]. They were first cousins and their families – all peasants who farmed smallholdings – had lived in the small village of Jafarabad for centuries. Jafarabad is 20 kilometres from the desert city of Yazd, now a UN heritage site but at that time a poor and undistinguished town which had barely changed in centuries. The same was true of Jafarabad.

Shirin

Yazd was on the edge of two vast and hostile deserts – the Dasht-e Kavir (Great Salt Desert) to the north and the Dasht-e Lut (Lut Desert) to the east and south-east. Yazd and its surrounding villages were the last settlements of any significance for 1000 km. The desert terrain was bleak – characterised by vast arid landscapes, salt flats, and curious geological formations. The landscape was punctuated by low-lying mountains and rocky outcrops, with sandy dunes, salt marshes, and sparse vegetation. But it was basically the same, whichever direction you faced.

The climate was harsh, with extreme temperature variations – intensely hot summers (sometimes reaching up to 50°C) and cold winters with below-freezing temperatures at night and snow on the higher plateaux.

And the winds would come rolling over the desert bringing sand that covered everything. Not sandstorms in the classic sense – though those also from time to time – but just a regular film of sand which crept into every nook and cranny. Indeed, for 20 or 30 years after the early to mid-1950s Jafarabad was abandoned to the sand and its houses were almost completely submerged. In recent years that has changed somewhat and some of the houses have been reclaimed. To live there, and more especially to pursue a life farming, was challenging and heartbreaking. But the land had been farmed for centuries, the owners over time removing rocks, arranging irrigation and making it possible to farm the fields.

Jafarabad itself was an unremarkable desert village of fewer than 100 houses, all very similar, constructed from adobe (mud and straw bricks, with their outer surfaces smoothed over) generally with flat and some with slightly domed roofs to resist the intense heat. These

Jafarabad in 1995 (above) and in 2025 (right) – note the sand up to the roofs

roofs were often part of the living, or rather the sleeping, area. Homes were usually organized around inner courtyards that provided a private, shaded area for family gatherings and domestic activities. The photos below are of Jafarabad when it had been abandoned, and of Faraj village today which is also close to Yazd and is very much as Jafarabad would have been before it was lost to the sand.

The house in which Shirin and Khorsand lived and in which Shahriar was born had been in the family for generations (remember that Shirin and Khorsand shared a grandparent, called Bahram) and was down one of the narrow streets which crisscrossed the centre of the village – narrow in order to keep the houses in shade during the summer and to stay warmer in winter. Like all the others it was built of mud bricks, typical of a desert town not just in Iran but around the world. It was modest – it had just one storey and was built around a courtyard, one of whose sides had a room with a stage-like platform protruding which was used for religious observances, and with rooms on three others some with whitewashed walls. There was also a kitchen area that contained a bread oven and a hearth for cooking, fuelled by twigs and brushwood. Outside was a toilet of sorts (essentially a hole in the

Faraj – a village near Yazd and very much as Jafarabad was previously

ground above a deep pit), whose contents were spread over fields as fertiliser and an additional lean-to which housed the small number of goats and sheep they kept for their milk, wool and occasionally meat. In the courtyard was a small pit for legs to work the pedals of the weaving loom set up above it, where cloth for simple clothes were produced from cotton and home spun wool, harvested from the family's sheep.

There was very little by way of furniture – bed rolls that were put away each morning, and a low table and two stools for guests, though the family would sit on the floor. There were, inevitably this being Iran, old rugs on the floor. And a shelf – made of mud, like everything else – with a picture of Zoroaster placed on it. Their meals consisted of produce which they had grown themselves – eggs, bread, vegetables like turnips, yoghurt and occasionally, when they slaughtered an animal, some meat though that was rare. All cooked in various herbs – fenugreek, coriander, mint and chives which they also grew.

Jafarabad was a village almost all of whose inhabitants were Zoroastrian, and as with other Zoroastrian villages, it contained a modest fire temple, the spiritual heart of Zoroastrian life, which nestled unobtrusively among other buildings, constructed like them of simple

House interior – Jafarabad

adobe and stone. These temples housed an ever-burning sacred flame, symbolizing purity and the eternal light of Ahura Mazda.

When they married Shirin was 14 and Khorsand 18. They had three children in quick succession. Katayoun was born in 1915 when Shirin was just 16 years old. Shahriar followed in 1916 and another son, Shirmard, followed in 1919. Perinatal mortality was high in Iran at the time – both for mothers and newborn – but Shirin and her babies thrived.

In 1919 typhus swept Iran ravaging the area around Yazd. It hit Jafarabad especially hard. Of the 60 or so families living there most experienced the loss of one or more family members. Shahriar lost his father and his sister Katayoun as well as Shirin's mother and her brother Mehraban. At the age of 20 Shirin was a widow, pregnant with her third child, and Shahriar and his soon-to-be born brother Shirmard were fatherless.

Shahriar's father had been a peasant farmer like generations before him. He had a small plot of land on which he grew pistachio trees and cultivated pulses and legumes, herbs, wheat and alfalfa for the small number of hens, sheep and goats they kept, together with other subsistence produce on which the family lived. They also grew poppies, which merchants sold on into India and which ended up in the hands of the British – and it is well-known what use the British made of the opium that this produced.

In the absence of modern pesticides, among the ruinous blights which made agriculture so hard were locusts and the cereal sap eating beetle, which could be surprisingly local in the devastation they would cause. The helplessness of seeing an entire year's crop being obliterated by a swarm of locusts against which there was no defence[2] drove families to despair. It did not happen often, but when such a disaster occurred it meant a year or two of great hardship and risked starvation for the family. And as might be imagined, in such a desert environment, one thing that Yazd and Jafarabad lacked was rainfall – it hardly ever rained. But they had water. Farming was only possible because of the remarkable Qanat system that brought water to desert villages like Jafarabad.

The Qanat System

The Qanat system played a critical role in sustaining agricultural productivity, supporting settlements, and providing water for domestic use in areas where surface water sources were scarce. It allowed access to groundwater from aquifers, replenished each year from snow melted from the nearby mountains, transporting it long distances to where it was needed for irrigation, drinking, and other uses. The water flowed along a gently sloping underground tunnel that tapped into an aquifer or water source deep beneath the earth, bringing water to the surface by gravity without the need for pumps. Once the water had reached the surface the channel along which water flowed was known as a Joo. And where water was available settlements developed, their names often suffixed with the word 'Abad', which means 'fertile' – hence 'Jafarabad' (the place that Jafar made fertile).

The Qanat system is not only a technological marvel but also an important part of Iran's cultural heritage. It allowed for the flourishing of agriculture and civilization in some of the harshest environments on earth. Cities like Yazd, and its surrounding villages, which are located in one of the driest regions of Iran, owe much of their survival and prosperity to the Qanat system, which facilitated the rise of large cities in desert regions, allowing Iranian culture, agriculture, and trade to thrive. It allowed, for example, mulberry trees to grow by the side of running streams in many local villages, whose leaves fed the silkworms which enabled the silk production for which Yazd was famous. These systems were so effective that they were adopted in other regions of the Middle East, North Africa, and even southern Spain.

Water management from a Qanat between agricultural fields was highly structured and regulated. In Jafarabad, as in most villages, the Qanat was a communal asset, and its water was shared by the farmers who either contributed to its construction and maintenance or had inherited rights to use its water. The system of distribution was designed to ensure fairness, maximize agricultural productivity, and sustain the water supply for future generations. Jafarabad, like other villages, had a paid Mirab, whose duty it was to oversee the amount of irrigation time each landowner should be allocated according to what had been paid by each. The time measuring system was a water clock which consisted of a bucket of water with a bowl which had 30-minute markings around it. The bowl's centre was pierced allowing to it float on the surface until the water bowl's inside edge started to become submerged against the 30-minute markings.

This ingenious old watering system had its origins long, long ago and had been in use for over 2,500 years. The other thing that this watering system permitted was the flourishing of walled gardens – 'Baghs' – in the middle of the desert. Shahriar and his family did not possess a Bagh, but there were three or four in Jafarabad and they had a friend who possessed one. Shahriar spoke lyrically about the pleasure afforded by the Bagh, and the sadness occasioned when it

Baghs

Baghs were an important cultural tradition – based on a traditional garden design that originated in ancient Persia and which have had a lasting influence on garden and carpet design worldwide.

These gardens are enclosed by high walls, offering protection from the harsh desert climate as well as a sense of privacy. The walls help maintain a microclimate inside the garden, keeping it cooler and more humid, and the gardens are celebrated for their geometry, symbolism, and use of water, creating a structured, serene space that contrasts with the often-harsh surrounding landscape.

The earliest known Baghs were introduced in the reign of Cyrus the Great in the 6th Century BC, and the most famous in more recent times were (and remain) in Shiraz and Isfahan. When the Greeks encountered these impressive gardens, they adapted the Old Persian word "pairidaeza", which means an enclosed space or garden, into their language as "paradeisos". Over time, this term entered Latin as "paradisus" and eventually made its way into English as "paradise," coming to signify a perfect, blissful place, full of colour and perfumed flowers often used in religious contexts to mean heaven.

Individuals and families of even modest means often had their own Bagh where they could relax, and entertain friends among formally presented flower gardens, and fruit trees and running water.

was devastated by a swarm of locusts (which miraculously did not do harm to his family's field).

The Qanat system was not infallible. Water was a constant cause for anxiety, and in due course the water source diminished. In 1955 the water completely dried up – the stream (Joo) that ran the length of the village stopped flowing, but there remained some water in the reservoir which was accessible for a while until that ran out too – and, as has already been mentioned, the village was abandoned. What was true for the inhabitants of Jafarabad was true of many of those living nearby. Economic necessity largely drove a diaspora from the villages and into the towns or further afield – many went to India as is discussed below.

Shirin, with two small children to raise, could not take over the work of her late husband. She relied very heavily on her father Jamshid, himself only in his early 40s, to help shoulder the burden.

Even the little Shahriar was not spared his share of responsibility, and from the age of five he was expected to help in the fields, and he recalled in particular that it was his job from time to time to divert the flow of the Joo that fed his family's smallholding, regulating the provision of water to one or other part of the field.

At the age of six Shahriar began attending the village school. He would get up early most mornings – in the summer he, his mother, brother and grandfather would sleep on the roof of their house and in the winter, when it could be very cold at night in the desert, they slept inside the house huddled up together. He would do his duties in the field and trot off to school with his slate

Jamshid – Shirin's father, Shahriar's grandfather

and chalk and with his sheepskin on which he would sit on the floor of the classroom. There were just two classrooms in the school – a school whose pupils were aged between six and 12 – where he learned the basics of reading, writing and elementary arithmetic, and proved to be a keen and intelligent pupil.

Among the 300 or so inhabitants of Jafarabad, only two families were Muslim, both recent converts – the prizes for conversion were great and the penalties for failure to convert greater, as is described below – and so the school was for Zoroastrian children. We do not know this but we think it very likely that the school was free, founded and funded by Parsee benefactors (Indian Zoroastrians of Iranian descent), as were schools in other Zoroastrian settled villages.

In his second year the school was visited by the senior Zoroastrian priest (Dastur) for the parish[3]. This visit was keenly anticipated and on the day of his visit, as he arrived, he was greeted by children running excitedly from the school, Shahriar at their head. "Welcome to our school, we have been waiting eagerly for you to visit us and honour us with your presence". He chatted away to the Dastur who was impressed by his mature use of language and by his intelligence, and even more so when he attended the class and saw Shahriar's precocious ability. This Dastur – Dastur Shahbahram – was to be doubly significant in Shahriar's life, as will become apparent later in his story.

Dastur Shahbahram made enquiries and being told of Shahriar's difficult circumstances and believing that he showed promise which would not be fulfilled at the village school, over the next year arranged for Shahriar to attend the Marker[4] orphanage for Zoroastrian children in Yazd, where the education was at a different level. So from the age of eight Shahriar was removed from the Jafarabad village school and went as a boarder to the Marker orphanage school in Yazd.

Dosabahai Marker was an Indian Parsee, a businessman and philanthropist, who, having been made aware of the deplorable condition of many Zoroastrians in Iran, made substantial charitable donations for the establishment of welfare and educational facilities for Iranian Zoroastrians, especially in the cities of Yazd and Kerman, where the majority of Iranian Zoroastrians lived. In Yazd these included an orphanage school which opened in 1921, five years later Girls' and Boys' Primary Schools and a Boys' High School; and then, finally, in 1931 a Girls' High School. Shahriar was among the first to benefit from his charity.

Even at that time, Yazd was a busy and noisy city, and quite different from the village that Shahriar was used to. He had only been out of Jafarabad once before in his life – just one year previously, to Yazd. He was seven years old and had injured himself at play in the village. His injury had become infected and his family was concerned. The village had no doctor, but there was a Christian missionary medical centre in Yazd and so his grandfather took him there. Shahriar was placed on a donkey and his grandfather led him into the city and to the clinic – a walk of more than four hours each way (by donkey – on foot it was about three hours). For a sick child this will have been a truly exhausting experience, but with no other medical facilities available, that is what they had to endure. When they got to the centre of Yazd – approaching the bazaar – an angry bystander pushed Shahriar off the donkey saying that it was a sin that a Zoroastrian should be riding on a donkey and passing a Muslim on foot (it was clear from their clothes that they were Zoroastrians).

It is time at this point to explain the Zoroastrian religion and how things stood for Zoroastrians in Iran at the time.

With its roots back in the 2nd millennium BC, Zoroastrianism was the national religion in Iran until the Arab Muslim invasion of the 7th century AD, and is regarded as one of, if not the, first monotheistic religions in history, predating Judaism, Christianity, and Islam, on all of which Zoroastrianism has had a significant cultural and theological impact. The number of adherents to the religion had diminished substantially in Iran since the 7th century, and in the early 20th century they numbered no more than 10,000, the majority concentrated in the Yazd region. While numbers had increased to as many as 33,000 in the 1970s[5], since the 1979 revolution and the creation of the Islamic republic its numbers have dwindled to the point of extinction.

Up to the 1920s, Zoroastrians in Iran faced significant discrimination as a minority religious group in a predominantly Muslim society, especially under laws that privileged Islam. Reza Shah (see below) began to undo some of the systemic and official discrimination, but until that time – and indeed after, and until this day – some of these burdens continued to be borne by Zoroastrians and others of a minority religion.

Zoroastrians were considered dhimmis, or protected non-Muslim minorities, under Islamic law, which granted them limited rights but also second-class status. They were often viewed with suspicion by the Muslim majority and were treated as religiously impure (najes), which restricted their social interactions. In rural areas, Zoroastrians were sometimes barred from using public water sources or participating fully in communal life. They faced restricted access to economic opportunities and were required to pay higher taxes, including the jizya tax, a special levy on non-Muslims, intended not only as a means of raising money, but as an incentive for Zoroastrians to convert to Islam These hardships were taken up by the Parsee Amelioration Society for the Improvement of the Conditions of Zoroastrians in Persia in the mid-19th-century, and in the late 19th century the jizya was eliminated, paid off as a lump sum to the Iranian government by Parsees in India.

Zoroastrianism, like other minority religions, could not be freely practised in public. Their adherents were restricted from holding public religious ceremonies, and faced pressure to convert to Islam. Religious texts and symbols were sometimes confiscated, and public expressions of Zoroastrian culture were curtailed.

In certain areas, especially in rural regions, Zoroastrians faced violence and intimidation from religiously motivated groups. Attacks on Zoroastrian homes, land confiscation, and even occasional forced conversions were reported (including the grandmother of the founder of the Parsee Amelioration Society for the Improvement of Conditions for Iranian Zoroastrians, referred to above), and official action against such incidents was rare. Even where conversions were not forced, the incentives to convert were strong. For example, if one child in a family converted to Islam then they would inherit the entire estate of deceased parents – their Zoroastrian siblings would receive nothing. At a more mundane level, our mother Laal reports how once when she went with her mother to market, and put down a fruit that she had picked up the stallholder berated them for their "unclean" handling of the fruit.

In his 1905 book *Five Years in a Persian Town*, which describes his life in turn-of-the-century Yazd where he was a missionary, Napier Malcolm writes:

> *The atmosphere of the town seems to have resembled, as indeed it still resembles, that of a preparatory school for little boys. Up to 1895 no Zoroastrian was allowed to carry an umbrella. After 1895 there was a strong prohibition upon eyeglasses and spectacles. Up to 1885 they were prevented from wearing rings. Their girdles had to be made of rough canvass. Up to 1896 they were obliged to twist their turbans instead of folding them. Up to about 1898 only brown, grey and yellow were allowed for body garments. There was also a prohibition against white stockings, and up to about 1880 they had to wear a special kind of peculiarly hideous shoe with a broad turned up toe. Up to about 1880 they had to wear tights and knickers instead of trousers. Up to 1891 all Zoroastrians had to walk in town, and even in the desert they had to dismount if they met a Muslim of any rank whatsoever. Their houses (and that of Jews), and the surrounding walls, had to be built so low that the top could be reached by a Muslim with his hand extended. The walls had to be splashed with white around the door. Double doors were forbidden as were rooms containing three or more windows. Up to 1870 they were not allowed schools for their children.*

Malcolm's account is repeated here at length because it provides a graphic backdrop to an important element of the environment in which Shahriar lived. Yazd was known for being especially insular and intolerant towards Zoroastrians. While it is also true that the incidents and discrimination such as are described here became less common as time went on, and indeed official measures – laws that forbade rank discrimination – were passed, the enforcement of those laws in a place like Yazd was patchy to say the least, and Zoroastrians continued to face barriers in business, and property rights were sometimes limited or unenforced.

So this was the religion practised by Shahriar and his family, and which shaped the environment in which he was growing up. Zoroastrians even had their own language – Dari – which had its variations, even between villages, and which non-Zoroastrians could not understand[6]. Indeed, some of the older Zoroastrians even in Shahriar's time could not speak Farsi. There remain a small number to this day for whom Dari is their first language. Their religion permeated their lives, and Zoroastrians, were reminded – by others but also by themselves, and for both better and for worse – of their culture and religion.

Shahriar received the news that he was going to go away to school with equanimity, excitement even. He did not seem fazed by the fact that he was going to be torn away from his familiar background and his family and begin a new life in the big city among strangers. That seems to have been a more general trait with him. His life took many unexpected turns throughout, but he took each more or less in his stride.

One thing specifically that he remembered was the excitement with which he made the journey to Yazd to be fitted out for the new school. It was an orphanage school, and so the children attending can be expected to have come from impoverished backgrounds, but as remains common in the Middle East in particular, the cost of education was something that families expected to contribute towards. And so in this case his family paid for the shirt and matching jacket that comprised the Marker orphanage school uniform. The uniform also included a Kepi (peaked) hat, which Shahriar remembered gave him great pride and pleasure. Kitted out in his new uniform he looked smarter than any child in his village and he was eager to wear it when

Zoroastrianism

Key elements of Zoroastrian belief include:

- *Good Thoughts, Good Words, Good Deeds: This moral triad is a guiding ethical principle, encouraging followers to live righteously and make morally good choices.*
- *Dualism: Zoroastrianism teaches that we have choices – the good course of action and the bad. And it illustrates this by teaching that the supreme creator, Ahura Mazda, created two opposing energies between which humans have to choose in their everyday lives.*
- *Environmental Stewardship, emphasising the sanctity of earth, water, fire, and air.*

No account of Zoroastrian practices is complete without some reference to the Towers of Silence, where traditionally Zoroastrians – both in Iran and in India – took their dead after the religious rites had been completed, to be devoured by vultures. That is a practice that may seem strange today, but which is in keeping with the Zoroastrian belief that earth, air, fire and water should be unpolluted. Towers of Silence no longer function in Iran, because of the dearth of vultures (where in any case the practice was banned in the 1960s), and in India numbers have been decimated as a result of the use of drugs in animal feed, and the practice has been much reduced.

There were other practices. For example, Zoroastrians realised the particular intelligence of dogs – one practice was to use a dog to confirm whether somebody had died: they placed a morsel of bread on the body, and if the body was still alive, the dog would not eat it. And the families of priests would not begin a meal until the youngest child had put out some of the food for the neighbourhood dogs. Also, Zoroastrians had their own calendar and festivals, including NoRuz which was celebrated throughout Iran – and still is despite an early attempt by the Islamic regime to ban it.

he returned to Jafarabad, but was forbidden from doing so lest the clothes be spoiled before he had even started at school.

So in January 1924 Shahriar left home to make the trip back to Yazd to start his new school life, accompanied by his grandfather. He did not remember feeling nervous, only excited.

It might be thought difficult for a child of that age to be taken from a remote village and his home and placed in an orphanage in a busy and noisy city, far away, without any prospect of seeing his family and having to live among strangers. But by all accounts, Shahriar thrived, and had no complaints. Indeed, in some ways it could be that life was actually much better than it had been. No more getting up at the crack of dawn and working in the fields before going off to school and being required to work in the fields as well after returning home. He was able to spend his days studying – which he did well – and being with similar aged children and enjoying the company he had few complaints.

Not that life at the orphanage was simple. As at home, he was required to wake early, and unlike at home, he would have been sleeping in a room with other children, not of his choosing. He would have had to prepare for the day rapidly – but washing in cold water was no hardship as he was used to that, and the toilets, elementary though they might have been, were no different from those that he had been used to. It might have been different if he had been orphaned at an older age and had come to the orphanage after he had become longer accustomed to a different way of life.

In the past, orphanages and indeed all elementary schools (though it has to be noted that village schools were an extreme rarity) were often religious foundations, created as a result of charitable donations. But the reforms of Reza Shah in the early 1920s had required that elementary education should be compulsory and secular and so the instruction that the children received was basic reading, writing, mathematics and some history – one of the objectives was to instil a sense of national pride, identity and patriotism. Shahriar found the lessons easy. Although the classes were better differentiated than at his village school where there were only two classes for children between the ages of 6 to 12, he had no difficulty keeping up, and was ahead of the rest of his class. That gave him a certain amount of kudos and stature when it came to homework and helping other children prepare for the next day's lessons.

One other thing that all schools instilled from a very young age was a love of literature, and poetry in particular. From the youngest age children were required to learn passages of the great Persian poets – Ferdowsi, Hafez, Rumi and Khayyam. And that continues to this day. One of the notable things about Iranians is the way they will find an apt couplet to illustrate any situation.

Discipline was strict, and Shahriar was a precocious and probably naughty boy; so he received his share of punishment, which was invariably physical – but he seemed to regard this as acceptable and normal, and did not complain. Indeed, physical punishment was not seen as an outrage. When Laal, his future wife, undertook a period of apprenticeship as a household maid (as young girls did in order to induct them into the mysteries of running a household) she recalls the master of the house removing his belt and using it to beat her 2 or 3 times – not especially gently – because of some minor infraction. The same would undoubtedly have been the case at school, but not unexpected and would have been shrugged off, and certainly appears to have been by Shahriar.

Although Shahriar was not expected to work as regularly as he had been expected to do in the fields at home, he was nevertheless expected to do his share of chores, maintaining the institution, and also doing some work in the gardens which provided some of its food. But there was also time to play, and being surrounded as he was by children of a similar age, Shahriar appeared to enjoy the orphanage for that as well. Games were simple. If they were lucky, they would have a football that they could kick around. More often it was a game of five stones, for which no equipment was required other than six pebbles.

The children were not allowed home at weekends – in large part because most of the children had no home to go home to. But from time to time – at the end of term and on public and religious holidays, Shahriar would be accompanied back to his village by his grandfather or by another relative, where his mother would tearfully greet him, ruing the day that she had allowed her oldest son to be removed from her. She had another son – Shahriar's brother Shirmard – but her oldest and most precious had gone. Shahriar seems to have been unmoved by these displays, in the same way as he was later, when his mother lived with him.

Shirin was not an easy person. But that is not surprising, considering the losses that she had suffered and the poverty in which she was living. But in case it should seem surprising that she allowed Shahriar to leave home and go to school in Yazd, leaving her alone with his brother and her father, it should be recalled that Iran – and in particular a village like Jafarabad – was a largely patriarchal society despite the Zoroastrian insistence on the equality of men and women. Decisions about such things – even about her own son – would predominantly have been taken by male relatives, who, one assumes, saw that attending the Marker orphanage school, and especially as recommended by the chief Dastur to the area, was without question the right thing for Shahriar to do.

Anyway, Shahriar thrived at the school, was one of the star pupils, and was noticed by the head teacher – Mirza Soroosh Lohrasb. Like Marker, who founded and funded the orphanage, Mirza Soroosh was a remarkable and selfless Zoroastrian. As a young graduate of the American College in Tehran, he could easily have got a high paying job in industry or administration. Instead, persuaded by Marker, he went to Yazd and served the school community for 30 years. Shahriar owes him a huge debt of gratitude for the care that he took of him, and continued to take during the next phases of his life.

During his time at the Marker orphanage school – in 1925 when Shahriar was nine – Reza Shah who had just become king and was determined fundamentally to modernise and reform Iran, introduced a law that required everybody in Iran to have a surname. Until then surnames existed but patchily and in a village like Jafarabad nobody had a surname – people were simply known by where they lived or the family that they came from. Until then Shahriar was simply Shahriar-e-Khorsand. What to do with the children in the orphanage? The head teacher was required to ensure that each child in his care had a surname. Mirza Soroosh took this in hand and suggested Bekhradnia – one might have hoped that he would have suggested something simpler but Bekhradnia was suggested, comprising three parts "beh", "kherad" and "nia" whose composite meaning was "Child of one with wisdom". Shahriar had no reason to disagree and so that was the name that was chosen as the family surname. That is how his family has come to have a name that most outside Iran find unpronounceable[7]. Unfortunately, at the same time, the headman of Jafarabad also regarded it as his duty to ensure that everybody in the village had a surname and so it came about that Shahriar's mother had a different surname to Shahriar – in her case Shirmardi, the name adopted also by his brother Shirmard so two brothers with the same parents came to have different surnames.

Under the education reforms of Reza Shah there were end of year exams which pupils had to pass before they could pass on to the next year. Shahriar sailed through these and at the age of 14, among the oldest boys in the school, he passed his 14-plus exam and that was it. The school did not provide education beyond the age of 14, so he was obliged to leave. That was not a happy moment for him. He had no obvious future path to pursue, but he was determined not to return to the village life that he had come from.

Passage to India

At the age of 14 when the time came to leave the Marker Orphanage School Shahriar's options appeared extremely limited. Having mixed with boys from very different backgrounds and having been identified at the Marker school as well as his village school as a pupil of exceptional ability, he was reluctant to return to village life and spend the remainder his life as his father, and his ancestors prior to him, had done. He wanted something better.

As has already been mentioned, there was something of a history of Zoroastrians, especially from the Yazd area, emigrating to India to seek a better life. For centuries – beginning soon after the Arab conquest – they had done so, and the fact that this diaspora was still a feature in the 20th century is not surprising. Life was hard, especially for peasant farmers who found it increasingly difficult to eke out what was already a difficult living, as the conditions in which they operated deteriorated over time. Indeed, Mirza Soroosh, the head of the orphanage (and in due course of all the Marker establishments in Yazd), had himself spent some time in India and was married to a Parsee woman, and he encouraged Shahriar to consider going to India to see what he could achieve there.

The Zoroastrian diaspora to India had included in its number some family members, one of whom – Aunt Soltan – was his mother's half-sister, who had lived in the next village. She, like Shahriar's mother Shirin, had married young, and had three daughters and three sons. But life for the family became progressively harder, and they decided, like so many others before them, to join the Zoroastrian diaspora to India. Initially at least the move did not lead to a pot of gold, but the family survived, and eventually found their feet. Her sons all found work in Iranian tea-houses – Iranian tea houses or Chai khaneh were all well-known in Bombay[8] and remain so to this day – and Esfandiar, one of Shahriar's cousins and the son of his mother's full sister, later married the daughter of the owner of the chain of cafes in which he worked. He rose to manage and later own the entire chain which exists to this day, serving wonderful fruit drinks, chai, light snacks, meals and pastries, and that family's future was secure. Shahriar communicated with Aunt Soltan and she readily agreed to welcome him, to arrange employment for him and to arrange an education as well. So at the age of 14 Shahriar decided to travel to Bombay to seek his fortune there.

But how to arrange to go to India? There was no doubt that his aunt would help him once he was there, but the logistics – and the cost – of the travel were daunting.

Shahriar first set about obtaining the money, which proved less difficult than might have been anticipated. But the money was not everything. For a 14-year-old from a small village, albeit someone who had lived in the city of Yazd for several years, arranging the travel, let alone the prospect of living in a foreign country, was a major undertaking. Fortunately for Shahriar, there was a wealthy Zoroastrian merchant, Mr Jehanian, from whom Shahriar sought assistance: although he did not know him, he made contact through acquaintances. Mr Jehanian was well-versed in the modes of travel between Yazd and Bombay – which by now was the centre of the Parsee community. Shahriar approached Mr Jehanian and obtained an audience whose outcome surpassed his expectations. Mr Jehanian agreed to lend him some money, but also helped Shahriar devise a budget for the trip and to plan the route and other practical logistics.

As a trader importing and exporting goods (including, poppies and the product of poppies – though it should be borne in mind that there was no shame attached to this at the time and in the environment we are speaking of), Mr Jehanian had agents travelling regularly to buy and sell, and one of them – Ali, whose surname we do not know – was due to travel from Yazd to Bombay in April 1930, via the Gulf port of Bandar-e-Abbas. With Ali being one of Mr Jehanian's employees there was trust between them – a trust that proved to be the saving of Shahriar. He put Shahriar under Ali's care who was to deliver him to his aunt after they had arrived in Bombay.

Shahriar had written to Aunt Soltan telling her of his hopes, and she had agreed to take him in. Family solidarity and mutual help was a normal and expected feature of life in the Zoroastrian community: and in the same way as her family had been received and helped to settle in Bombay by previous emigrants from Yazd, so she had no hesitation in agreeing to receive and welcome Shahriar. But it was now many weeks since he had heard from her and although he could have no certainty that the arrangement stood, he decided to proceed anyway. Ali booked them both on a cargo ship bound from Bandar-e-Abbas to Bombay. The day was set and the die cast.

The journey to Bombay was long and arduous. It meant first getting to Bandar-e-Abbas port on the Persian Gulf and from there getting a cargo ship that was destined for Bombay. Bandar-e-Abbas was not the nearest port – that was Bushir which was 500 km away compared to the 700 kms to Bandar Abbas. But Bandar-e-Abbas was larger, and had more freight traffic (something that Shahriar had reason to be grateful for as his initial plans had to be revised) – and there was better transport to Bandar-e-Abbas from Yazd.

The adventure on which Shahriar embarked cannot be overstated. First Jafarabad and then Yazd were the bounds of his experience. Now he set off on what must have seen like a daunting adventure, and he several times contemplated abandoning the idea – but dispelled these doubts when he reminded himself of the limited future that awaited him in Jafarabad

So on an unknown date in April 1930 they set out. The journey to Bandar-e-Abbas port was tortuous. First, they hitched a ride on a lorry going as far as Kerman, and from Kerman they had to take a bus that was due to go to all the way to Bandar Abbas. They journeyed through strange and inhospitable countryside – the desert is unremittingly bleak – rocky, in part sandy and invariably hot during

Dasht-e-Kavir (Kavir Desert)

the day – in fact countryside that Shahriar was used to. They arrived in Kerman without incident later the same day as their departure, and immediately transferred to a scheduled bus due to arrive in Bandar-e-Abbas three days later.

At that time – as today – long-distance buses were organised with two drivers, one of whom slept while the other drove. This was not a great recipe for safety, and periodically and regularly on the roads were skeletons of buses that had crashed. Shahriar's bus did not crash, but more than a day away from Bandar-e-Abbas it broke down and could not be repaired without a new part. Fortunately for the passengers, the breakdown occurred close to a village where, for a price which had not been factored into Shahriar's budget, the passengers were able to obtain some shelter from the heat of the day and the cold of the night. The driver got a lift to the nearest town of any size, returned with a mechanic who managed to fix the problem and after two days of delay they were on their way again.

They arrived in Bandar-e-Abbas shortly after the cargo ship on which they were booked had departed. This was potential disaster –

Dasht-e-Lut Aleut (Lut Desert)

Shahriar had only enough money for the trip on which he was booked – he had spent the money and could not afford to pay for a second fare. Ali saved him, and agreed to loan Shahriar the money for the second voyage, as well as some living expenses while they were marooned. As collateral Shahriar gave a gold chain that he carried round his neck (possibly a Fravahar, which is the winged symbol of the Zoroastrian religion – which has become a symbol worn by increasing numbers of modern Iranian youths, as a silent protest against the regime, and a way of harking back to the pre-Islamic history of Iran). But in any case, Ali was in a bind, as he could hardly abandon a 14-year-old 700 km from home with no money to survive. He bought them both a second boat ticket, confident in the knowledge that he would be repaid, if necessary by his employer. And indeed, Shahriar earned enough in India to redeem the necklace and repay the loan when Ali returned to Bombay on a future trip.

It was eight days before they found another boat willing to take them from Bandar-e-Abbas to Bombay. In the meantime both Ali and Shahriar found some casual work in the docks and lodged in a seaman's hostel. But eventually, more than a week after their scheduled departure Shahriar and Ali took a cargo ship carrying dried fruit from Bandar-e-Abbas to Bombay. It was a terrible trip. The sea was calm but Shahriar was horribly seasick – and travel sickness was an affliction that he suffered from throughout his life. He didn't eat for three days – although he and Ali had bought Nan-e-Sangak – unleavened bread cooked on heated pebbles – cheese and onions (traditional fare for a long-distance voyage in Iran); and although he drank water, much of the water that he drank was brought up. But after three days they arrived in Bombay.

Ali knew Bombay well and certainly knew the Persian tea cafés. On 1 May 1931 Shahriar arrived at Aunt Soltan's who greeted him warmly and took him home where he met two of his six cousins, Sarvar and Dowlat. The following day Shahriar began working in the kitchens of one of Bombay's tea cafés, collecting and washing glasses.

Aunt Soltan also arranged for Shahriar to attend a local school, insisting that he should at least learn English which was widely spoken in India at the time and would be necessary if Shahriar was to make his way successfully in India. We do not know if she paid for his schooling or if the school was free.

The school was a considerate idea but Shahriar resented it because – largely down to his poor, even non-existent, English and inability to speak any of the local languages – he was put into classes with children up to 3 years younger than himself. He was already tall and adolescent, and the children with whom he was classed were much younger. Nor did he find the work that he was set to do in the café agreeable. He did not see how he was going to make his fortune in India, he was homesick, became resentful and he developed uncontrollable nosebleeds. These were never diagnosed but may have had something do with the moist atmosphere of Bombay, which was completely alien to him – the contrast with the arid atmosphere of the Iranian desert could not have been more marked. He never found out their cause, but when he returned to Iran his nosebleeds stopped.

Bombay tea cafés

The contemporary Indian restaurants being spawned across the UK under the name of "Dishoom" are a conscious attempt to replicate the atmosphere and decor – if not the cuisine – of the Irani Tea Houses in Bombay. To quote from "Dishoom – from Bombay with love", published by Bloomsbury Publishing and written by Shamil Thakrar, Kavi Thakrar and Naved Nasir:

"19th-century Bombay is often and rightly described as a cosmopolitan city, but eating out was uncommon and almost always segregated. Religions had strong and specific prescriptions on diet, with caste an additional division... The Irani cafés, opened by outsiders, simply could not hold any such biases. They quietly subverted all the rules by welcoming allcomers...

And they were affordable. A few piastre could buy you a cup of chai and a bun maska or a biscuit. Over time, many local Irani Tea Houses became reliable places for a cheap, sustaining meal. They also became meeting and relaxing places for the great number who lacked the luxury of space at home (or even those, like hookers, who were shunned elsewhere).

They played a significant role in enabling women and children to participate in eating out by incorporating family rooms or cabins (which also had the unintended benefit of sheltering illicit liaisons). In this way, these cafés set up by immigrants became Bombay's first real public eating and drinking places. If Bombay was already full of all kinds of people, Irani cafés further helped to mix them physically in the same spaces and helped enhance the cosmopolitan culture of the city. When people break bread together, barriers break down."

We know little of the day-to-day experiences of Shahriar while in Bombay, but there is one facet of his experience which stands out, and which caused his children great amusement. It must be remembered that Shahriar came from an extremely conservative environment where sex was barely acknowledged let alone on display, and where he had little or no experience or knowledge of girls. He had no sisters who brought home friends, and his experience of schools was entirely of all-male company.

So when, both in the workplace and in public spaces, he was confronted with semi-nudity (as he will have seen it), voluptuous displays and sexual images, he was utterly taken aback. What he saw was an apparently unrestrained display of female bodies (bare midriffs under bright eye-catching saris, compared to the very strict and austere dress of women in Iran); and exaggerations of beauty, whereas in Iran beauty was for the most part concealed. He barely knew where to look.

He was quite flummoxed. He was 15 years old and undoubtedly experiencing emotions and stirrings, the confusion and longings common to most 15-year-old boys. Even worse were the sensuous dancing with flirtatious eyes, the Hindu temples with unabashed overt sexual sculptures; the shrines with lingams and yonis on full display; and the gods – these were gods whom Hindus worshipped! – using their multiple arms for unspeakable activities. One can only imagine his shock, horror, but also prurient interest. He was, after all, a 15-year-old boy embarking on manhood.

The other thing of course which he never discussed was whether he formed relationships with girls while working at the teahouse. He would certainly have had encounters with girls – apart from anything else his aunt had three daughters who themselves would have had friends. But whether these played any part in Shahriar's life we do not know. We do know that one of them at least found him attractive[9].

One other notable fact about Shahriar's stay in India is that he fell under the influence of a prominent spiritual leader – a guru called Mehr Baba who over time became guru to many hundreds of thousands of followers in six continents.

Mehr Baba's spiritual teachings were unremarkable – they probably differed in detail from other spiritual gurus, but the details seem immaterial.

Mehr Baba

Mehr Baba came from a Zoroastrian family from Khoramshah – a village very close to Yazd and not far from Jafarabad, where Shahriar's younger aunt Morvarid lived. Enduring the sort of poverty and hopelessness that afflicted so many others from a similar background, Mehr Baba's mother and father had followed the well-worn path, emigrating to Western India some years previously, in the late 19th Century.

Mehr Baba's teachings included the claim that he was the Avatar of his age (God in a human form); and that the goal of all life is to realize the absolute oneness of God, from whom the universe emanated as a result of the whim of unconscious divinity to know itself as conscious divinity. In pursuit of consciousness, evolution of forms occurs in seven stages: stone or metal, vegetable, worm, fish, bird, animal, and human. Every individualized soul, he taught, must experience all those forms in order to gain full consciousness. Once consciousness is attained, the burden of impressions accumulated in those forms prevents the soul from realizing its identity with God. To gain that realization, the individual must traverse an inward spiritual path, eliminating all false impressions of individuality and eventuating in the knowledge of the "real self" as God.

It seems doubtful whether many of his followers – or indeed the authors of this biography – grasped the full meaning of his philosophy. But what was remarkable about him – and what probably impressed his followers most – is that from the age of 31 until he died 44 years later, he was silent: he did not utter a word. He communicated first by using an alphabet board and later by unique hand gestures which were interpreted and spoken out by one of his disciples.

Considering that he travelled extensively, including to Europe and North America, and had meetings with celebrities wherever he went, it seems unlikely that he managed all this without speaking, but that apparently is so. We know very little about Shahriar's relationship with Mehr Baba or his movement, but he spoke very positively about him and about the influence that he had, and he did once or twice mention that he had seen him in his dreams.

It turns out not to be surprising that Shahriar was a follower of Mehr Baba in his youth. We have learned that his aunt Soltan, who received him in Bombay and so generously looked after him, was herself a devoted follower and in fact spent a significant part of her life living in Mehr Baba's ashram near Pune. And, perhaps as significant, Shahriar's mother Shirin kept images of Mehr Baba in her house in pride of place next to the picture of Zoroaster – it turns out that she too was a follower, whatever that might have meant. It could even be that one of Shahriar's motivations for going to India was precisely to be able to visit Mehr Baba, though that is something he never admitted to.

Shahriar told of his early adherence to Mehr Babar without any apparent embarrassment, though as a Zoroastrian Shahriar learned to tell the truth and act morally. He retained those characteristics throughout his life. He was the most upright man, and uncompromising in his adherence to what he believed was right, sometimes to a fault and his own detriment. But those were not uniquely characteristics of Mehr Baba or his teachings. It could just be that at the age of 14 he was star struck.

So after only a year in India, which was not a happy one, Shahriar decided to return to Iran. He had no hesitation in arranging his passage back, once again punctuated by seasickness, and under his own steam he returned to Iran. While in India, working as a glass washer, he had saved a certain amount of money. He had no expenditure while in India: his Aunt Soltan very generously accommodated and fed him, and perhaps paid for his schooling. So he was able to repay the merchant Mr Jehanian the loan he had given him at the outset, having already repaid the costs incurred by Ali on his behalf.

Teenage years

On returning from India, disappointed and virtually destitute, Shahriar had earned enough to repay his debts to Mr Jehanian who had loaned him money for the voyage, and to those of his relatives who had done so as well. But he had no job, no prospects and was once again responsible for his family.

This middle period of Shahriar's life – from the time he returned from India until his service in Kurdistan and Azerbaijan in his 20s – is something of a blur and we have little by way of information. The bare bones that we know are as follows.

Having returned from India Shahriar had no firm plans for his future, but one thing he did know was that he wanted to complete his education as far as possible, believing that education was the key to a bright future. None of his contemporaries in Jafarabad had done so.

The Shah at the time – Reza Shah Pahlavi, who had been an Iranian military officer – had staged a coup against the preceding Qajar Ahmad Shah, and after a time as Chief Minister, founded the Pahlavi dynasty. He subsequently reigned as Shah of Iran from 1925 until he was forced to abdicate after the Anglo-Soviet invasion of Iran in 1941. Reza Shah had embarked on a series of reforms to drag Iran into the 20th century, much as Ataturk was doing in Turkey at about the same time. Among his reforms was an insistence on the secularisation of the public space – discontinuance of official discrimination against minority religions and also, significantly, major education reforms.

In future, school education was to be in three phases – primary, lower secondary and upper secondary – the first two of which were to be compulsory. It was that, in part, that gave Shahriar the opportunity to earn money immediately after returning from India. He once again consulted his mentor Mirza Soroosh who recommended that Shahriar should work as a teacher in an elementary school, something for which he would gladly recommend him, and a role which he thought he would have no difficulty performing.

So he obtained work as a teacher in a Zoroastrian elementary school (similar to the one he had attended briefly in Jafarabad), teaching children from the ages of 6 to 12 – some of them not much younger than himself. In fact, he obtained jobs in two schools 12 km apart, one in the morning and one in the afternoon. He told how having taught in the local school in the morning, he used to cycle 12km to a school in a different village in the afternoon and home again each day, and then spend the evenings both preparing the next day's lesson and also preparing himself for the end of year exams for 15, and then 16-year-olds. It was tough. At least he had a bicycle. We were told by contemporaries that his was the first, and for a while the only, bicycle in the village, and it enabled him to get to and from work. It was exhausting, and for two years he worked extremely hard.

Some subjects he had no problems preparing for and teaching: he was especially knowledgeable about literature, poetry and history. Others he had real difficulty with, mathematics in particular, where he struggled to teach children some of whom were obviously more able than he was at the subject. But he coped, brought in an income, and enabled the family to survive.

One of the schools was in a village called Nasrabad, which was close to Yazd, and had by now been incorporated within the expanding city. At the same time, life in Jafarabad was becoming increasingly difficult, and Shirin, her father and his brother Shirmard were finding it harder to scrape together a living from the land: recent years had seen exceptionally hot summers, and the availability of water was becoming a problem (which in due course was to be so severe as to cause the stream to dry up, and force the virtual abandonment of the village). Shahriar never really described his relationship with his brother, and we do not know what he did after Shahriar left his village home, but Shahriar brought his mother to live with him in Nasrabad leaving Shirmard and Shirin's father to look after affairs in Jafarabad, something it would not be surprising if he resented.

Brother Shirmard, shortly before his disappearance

We know little about Shirmard. He was born in 1919, 3 years after Shahriar, and after his father's death. When Shahriar left home Shirmard became responsible for running the smallholding (in actual fact, Shirin's father did this initially). Shirmard was obliged to remain in Jafarabad while his brother Shahriar went first to school in Yazd and then to India – and then again when Shahriar did not come back to Jafarabad but remained working in villages around Yazd and finally went off to military Academy.

He was conscripted into the army (it seems that Iran had national service of some kind) at the age of 17 and was never seen or heard of again. It seems that he must have encountered some kind of accident and although enquiries were made, no official source or documentation was able to shed light on his disappearance. It could be the he simply decided to disappear, rather than have to retun to a life he found unappealing. Shahriar hardly ever spoke of his brother – not surprising really because they were virtual strangers. Shirmard would have been three when Shahriar went to the orphanage school and they rarely lived in the same house again. The above photo of Shirmard looks as though it may have been taken while he was on some kind of military duty, but nothing more is known.

As Shahriar was embarking on his 17th year, and preparing for his 16+ examinations, he consulted Mirza Soroosh again about his future. It was now that Mirza Soroosh suggested to him that a career as an officer in the armed forces was in principle open to him and would be highly respected, decently paid and would have excellent prospects. Such a career – at officer level – would hitherto have been inconceivable for somebody from Shahriar's background, but with all the changes taking place in Iran, and the reforms that had been put in place to make the country more meritocratic, it was not an unreasonable thing to aspire to.

Mirza Soroosh pointed out to Shahriar a notice in the fire temple offering a programme in Shiraz of military cadet training combined with academic study, leading to the competition for entry to the Military Academy. Scholarship places were available, depending on scores achieved in the 16+ examination. That provided an additional incentive for Shahriar to double down on his study and he passed the 16+ examination with flying colours – one of the highest scores in the country – and he easily achieved entry with a scholarship to the Cadet College.

This success was wonderful, but it was not unproblematic. Once again, Shahriar would leave his family and go away, this time not just to Yazd, not to India but to the big city – Shiraz where the Cadet College was based. His mother, Shirin, had left her home in Jafarabad only two years earlier to come to live with her older son – and now he was leaving her.

It must have been hard for him, but Shahriar was single-minded and did not give the matter a second thought. He could not acquiesce to Shirin's entreaties that he should return to the village and look after the family there. Indeed, he rather resented the fact that she would prefer him to live that life than the far greater possibilities that were now open to him.

Achieving entry to the Cadet College was competitive and was an achievement in itself. But the point of going to Cadet College was to achieve entry to the Military Academy – the Daneshkadeh-ye Afsari – that had been founded by Reza Shah in Tehran only a decade previously, and played an essential role in his efforts to create a modern army. But first he had to get through Cadet College, and do well in the competitive examinations for entry to the Military Academy.

Shiraz was a large and sophisticated city – quite a contrast with Yazd – but Shahriar already had experience of Bombay, which was certainly larger, and no less sophisticated. So the culture shock of moving from Yazd to Shiraz was not as great as it might have been. And in any case, by his account life in the Cadet College was very insular and there were not many opportunities to experience the city. They were expected to focus on academic work as in any secondary school preparing students for their school leaving certificate, but they were also being introduced to basic military concepts and techniques, which would have formed part of the entry exam to military college.

We know that he was very diligent in his studies and performed well, as he had done throughout his education hitherto, culminating in his success in the competitive examination for entry to the Military Academy. But we also know that he will have engaged in some of the behaviour and adventures typical of teenage boys.

He told, for example, of one occasion when he and a number of schoolmates went exploring roundabout and encountered a dervish[10] who was clearly intoxicated with drugs – probably opium, or hashish, which were common at the time. They were tempted to try some themselves, and one of the effects that Shahriar recalls is that it distorted perspectives hugely: what was in fact a small trickle of water near where they were sitting seemed to be a raging torrent, so much so that instead of stepping across it as he would have been able to do he took a flying leap, much to the amusement of some of his less intoxicated friends.

It would be an exaggeration to say that these were lost years, but these are certainly years about which we have little information concerning Shahriar's activities and development. What we do know though is that he succeeded in his school leaving certificate examinations and also succeeded in the competitive entry exam to military college. So, he passed out of Cadet College and entered the military academy at the age of 18, in 1934.

The army years: love and marriage

The level of education at the Academy was intended to be equivalent to that of a university degree, and the curriculum included military science, tactics, and subjects such as mathematics, engineering, and foreign languages. The graduates went on to serve in various branches of the armed forces, and were trained in more than one discipline (Shahriar spent time in the cavalry as well as the infantry).

Again, we do not have details of the three years that Shahriar spent in the Military Academy, but we have second-hand information from a contemporary[11] who became a colleague and friend (they shared a room both in the Academy and later in the army barracks to which they were posted in Tehran). He recounts how, as a result of an administrative error, Shahriar was obliged to spend three months on a preparatory (foundation) program before entry to the Academy proper during which he had to study material he had already studied and passed in the examination. When it was realised that a mistake had been made, he was transferred immediately to the Academy and given a year's seniority.

The same colleague also told how when, during Shahriar's final year, Reza Shah paid an official visit to the Academy Shahriar was selected to lead the parade that greeted him, and how he subsequently passed out of Military Academy in top place in his year. That Shahriar passed out top of his year is evidenced by the fact that he received the inscribed ceremonial sword, endorsed by the Shah, which was awarded each year to the highest performing passing out graduate. This can be seen in the photograph of Shahriar on parade and was left in the safekeeping of his wife Laal's younger brother Mehraban when Shahriar left Iran, remaining with him until the 1979 Islamic revolution. In the immediate aftermath of the revolution there was effectively a period of terror (which is far from over today),

Shahriar on parade (note the ceremonial sword)

with bands of revolutionaries searching houses for evidence of any relationship with or support for the Shah. Mehraban and his wife Simin, together with all other members of their families, destroyed anything that might indicate loyalty to the old regime, and that included disposal of the sword – we know not how or to whom. This account has been provided to us by Mehraban's wife Simin, currently living in Vancouver, who witnessed the sword and the concern that it raised prior to its disposal.

So it was that in 1937, at the age of 21, Shahriar passed out of the Military Academy and joined the infantry of the Imperial Army as a second lieutenant.

It cannot be overstated what an exceptional achievement it was for a village orphan with Shahriar's background to enter the Imperial Army as an officer. The Iranian Army officer corps had hitherto been considered an elite group effectively open only to aristocratic families. The Shah's meritocratic reforms had enabled Shahriar to be one of the very first to enter the Military Academy on his merits, now graduating with top honours as an officer in the Imperial Army. But

Shahriar, newly commissioned

he did not report of being in any way phased by this. By now he was used to being singled out.

Shahriar spent much of his time in barracks in Tehran, where his main duties included training both students at the Academy and ordinary soldiers in military matters – strategy and tactics, but also basic soldering. He also had to attend training courses himself which he found for the most part unrewarding, although training on new weaponry was of interest. He was an excellent shot and while it would be stretching what we know to say that he had become an expert horseman we do know that he spent time in the cavalry for which he had been trained during his time at the Military Academy, and indeed he was wearing jodhpurs in his wedding photograph. (The army reforms had not extended to superannuating the cavalry; though, given the dearth of mechanized equipment, horses and horse transport could still play a valuable role, especially in mountainous terrain). So he had two military allegiances, to the cavalry and also to the infantry.

He also had to go regularly on tours of duty to troublespots and on manoeuvres around Iran – generally to Kurdistan or Azerbaijan where there were already hints of insurgency. And in 1941, following the invasion of the Soviet Union by Nazi Germany, when the British and Soviets invaded Iran[12] in order to maintain control of the Iranian oil fields and also to create a land corridor for supplying the Soviet Union, he came within an ace of having to raise arms against the country that was eventually to be so welcoming and generous to him.

The British and Soviets had divided Iran into spheres of influence with the British taking the south and the Soviets the north. Shahriar was sent north to confront the Soviets, but little confrontation took place. The Iranians surrendered without much of a fight, concluding realistically that there was no point. It was as a result of this that Reza Shah was toppled, and sent into exile first in Mauritius and then South Africa, where he died; and his son Mohammed Reza Shah acceded to the throne.

Historically the Iranian officer corps, like the Russian on which it had been based, had consisted largely of aristocratic young men from wealthy families. It is no surprise then that a large part of their leisure time was spent gambling – playing cards and backgammon – though it is unlikely that Shahriar would have had the means to participate in any gambling; and within the barracks they drank tea, not alcohol – though they went regularly into town to drink and from time to time to smoke opium.

During 1944, when Shahriar was 28, a young doctor called Kaikhosrow Shahrvini used to visit the barracks. He was a few years younger than Shahriar, also Zoroastrian, and was employed as a doctor by the Air Force. They befriended each other, having their minority religion and language in common, but also because they discovered a remarkable point of coincidence. Kaikhsrow's father's name was Shahbahram – and was a Dastur. The very same Dastur Shahbahram who had identified Shahriar in the Yazd village school and arranged for him to attend the Marker Orphanage school in Yazd. Shahriar's entire career had been shaped by Kaikhosrow's father's actions 20 years ago.

Kaikhosrow was, like Shahriar, unmarried, and the question of marriage and marriage prospects arose in the course of their conversations. As young men might, they bantered about the eligibility of each, and what secret hopes they had.

Shahriar had not really given much thought to marriage. Although now an officer of the Imperial Army – a career traditionally reserved for the Iranian elite – he had never considered himself especially eligible, and had had no one to speak for him. He had always assumed that he might one day marry a village girl from back home, but had never taken the thought any further.

Kaikhosrow had developed a great attachment to and affection for Shahriar. "I have just the girl for you" he told him, or something similar. And he showed Shahriar a photograph of his middle sister Laal – possibly the photograph below.

Kaikhosrow's family (and therefore Laal's) was well known in the Zoroastrian community and highly regarded – family reputation was, and remains, highly valued in Iranian society. Moreover, they were from Yazd, which immediately created a bond with Shahriar.

Laal (right) and Homayoun (left)

Laal was a kind, gentle, generous and tolerant person. That is not surprising considering her family. Her father Shahbahram was a Zoroastrian priest and poet who travelled to India performing priestly duties (recently arrived Zoroastrians in India were very keen to have religious rituals and rites performed by Iranian priests) and having returned to Iran selling goods bought in India in order to supplement his income.

Her mother Gohar was illiterate, and her photograph at Appendix 1, is a fair representation of her as the gentlest of people. Laal had two brothers both of whom became doctors, and two sisters – one much older whom she did not really know. The other, Homayoun, was devoted to Laal and she to her, as will be seen below from the selfless way Laal cared for – virtually adopted – Homayoun's youngest and handicapped daughter.

Laal's father, Shahbahram, was determined that his daughters, no less than his sons, should receive the best education possible and should make the most of their lives. The Zoroastrian tradition does not differentiate between men and women (and from the very beginning, for example, women have been able to become priests). But education for girls was difficult in the absence of schools for girls. However, the Marker secondary school for girls opened in Yazd in 1926, when Laal was only six, and she was able to move seamlessly from primary to secondary school when she was 12 and then to upper secondary. Then, having graduated from secondary school she trained as a midwife in Tehran, where the family had moved in order to enable Kaikhosrow to train as a doctor. By the time she came to Shahriar's attention, she was pursuing her career as a midwife in a Zoroastrian-owned hospital in Tehran – unusual at that time. See Appendix 1 for more about Laal – who proved to be indispensable to Shahriar and the way his life progressed.

All of this – his good friend's recommendation of his sister, the photograph, Laal's background and achievement, the nature of the family and the remarkable coincidence of their father and his role in Shahriar's success so far – persuaded Shahriar that marriage to this accomplished and beautiful woman, and into this highly respected family, was something to be considered seriously. He did not take the bait immediately, but in early January 1945 he told Kaikhosrow that he would like to investigate whether marriage to his sister might be on the cards.

The tradition among Zoroastrians – as among a great many different cultures – is that when a man identifies (or has identified for him) a suitable wife, a well-established ritual is performed. Someone – normally a relative or someone with close ties to the family of the prospective groom and sometimes as the leader of a delegation – undertakes a formal visit to the potential bride's family, speaks in glowing terms of the prospective husband and makes a request for the hand in marriage of the girl, on his behalf. In the case of Shahriar the leader of the delegation was the wife of somebody whose family themselves had come from Jafarabad[13] and were known to Shahriar, and also to Laal's family. Shahriar also had an advantage in that Kaikhosrow would undoubtedly have sung his praises already. On the face of it there should have been no question: a handsome young Army officer who had achieved so much despite his very straitened origins and who had a reputation for honesty and virtue – and perhaps as importantly who had the support of the oldest brother – might objectively have been regarded as something to be jumped at. But it was not a simple as that.

The delegation arrived at Laal's house, and met Laal's family, led by Kaikhosrow as head of the family (Laal's father had died by now, and by tradition the oldest male became head of the family) and Laal's mother Gohar. Shahriar accompanied the delegation but stayed largely silent while the request was formally made. Laal and her younger sister Homayoun were not present, but peeped through a gap in the living room door that had been left ajar.

Laal was reticent. She was not sure that she was ready for marriage yet (that surely must be a reaction of many a young woman contemplating marrying somebody they had not met and knew little about), and anyway, she thought that his face was pockmarked. The pockmarked face was certainly a mistake, but an understandable one because Shahriar had spent some time recently on campaign duty in the mountains of northern Iran and his face, normally pale by Iranian standards, had darkened as a result. Anyway, she was not convinced but was persuaded to meet him, and give him a second chance.

So a further meeting was arranged this time between Shahriar and Laal, together with her entire family – surely a daunting prospect, but it went well. They met in an ice cream parlour and the conversation flowed between Shahriar, Kaikhosrow and Gohar; and by all accounts Homayoun mildly flirted with Shahriar during this discussion, catching his eye when she could and fluttering her eyelids when she did. She declared afterwards to Laal that Shahriar was the most handsome man she had ever seen, and that if Laal didn't marry her she would. Laal herself stayed silent through the whole encounter, not once looking directly at Shahriar, but by her accounts, casting sideways glances to confirm that not only was he not pockmarked but was indeed handsome. She later reported that she was especially struck by his eyes – hazel green, unusual in an Iranian, and deep and honest: terribly ironic in light of what was to follow.

Whatever it was – whether Homayoun's observation or her own, or the conclusion of her entire family that this was something to be seized and cherished – Laal relented and Shahriar received a positive response.

A few weeks later came the formal engagement – the 'ShiriniKhori' or exchange of sweetmeats, where each of the betrothed places sweets into the mouth of the other. We don't know who attended – on Shahriar's side, perhaps nobody. But that was it. The marriage was on.

Their engagement was traditional. They saw each other from time to time, and went out, but always chaperoned.

On one occasion they went cycling. Laal had learnt to cycle some time previously, but had not much practised, and the first time they went cycling together she clearly lost control of her bicycle, was unable to stop and was heading for an unpleasant accident. Shahriar, realising that there was a problem – not difficult, given the squeals and screams of terror coming from Laal – ran for all that he was worth after the runaway bicycle and managed to bring it to a halt before it reached the bend on which Laal would certainly have become detached from it. That event may have sealed Laal's view of Shahriar as a hero – but it could so easily have gone the other way.

One permitted activity was to go to the cinema together – always chaperoned, and more often than not by Laal's unmarried sister Homayoun and their younger brother Mehraban, who took care to sit several rows in front of them, and directly in front, to avoid impinging on their privacy. It is possible, but we think unlikely, that they held hands, sitting in their adjacent seats in the dark. It is though inconceivable that anything beyond that should have occurred.

They were engaged in February 1945, and the wedding took place just three months later in May 1945. The wedding was a subdued affair, in part because in the meantime Laal's younger sister, Homayoun, became betrothed to Bahman, one of the sons of Jamshid Jamshidian[14], a much respected and wealthy Zoroastrian. However, and sadly, before Shahriar and Laal's wedding one of his relatives died, and out of respect and in accordance with tradition, their wedding celebrations had to be restrained – more so than they would otherwise have been. We do not know the details, but we assume that there were no dancing or great festivities.

The wedding ceremony took place in Tehran's principal Fire Temple, officiated by the senior priest. As was traditional, heaps of sandalwood were burned and interminable prayers chanted by the priest. And then the marriage itself.

The priest asked Shahriar if he took Laal to be his wife, and he readily agreed. He then asked Laal if she took Shahriar as her husband, but she looked demurely down and was silent. He repeated the question, but still no reply. And then he repeated the question a third time, and in a small voice she said that she did. Her reticence was not because she had any doubts about marrying him. It was simply tradition that the bride should not seem eager – that she should display modesty and decorum. So they were married.

Laal and Shahriar wedding photo

Laal and Shahriar had rented a house owned by a fellow Zoroastrian Mr Farahmandi, and Shirin – Shahriar's mother – who had come from Yazd for the wedding and who was not especially happy to see, as she viewed it, her remaining child commandeered by another woman, moved in with them.

This was not a happy move for Laal. Shirin was jealous of her and did not like the time that Laal and Shahriar spent together. Specifically, for some reason, she did not like them leaving the house together to go to work. So they contrived to leave separately and to meet on the corner at the end of the road.

After their marriage, although Shahriar continued to be based in the barracks in Tehran, and so he and Laal were able to be together, he was also obliged to spend significant amounts of time in the field on manoeuvres, especially as the Kurdish and Azerbaijani insurrections were gathering pace. These rebellions were fomented by the Soviets who maintained their presence in northern Iran after the war and in breach of the treaty that divided Iran between Great Britain and the Soviet Union.[15] It was in July 1946, during one of the periods when Shahriar was based at the barracks in Tehran, that Laal became pregnant with their first child.

During Shahriar's absences Laal had to live alone with Shirin which was not easy – the tradition of the archetypal mother-in-law was well embodied in Shirin. But Laal was understanding of poor Shirin and her dreadful life experience to date, and accommodated her stoically.

Tragedy

During the mid-to-late 1940s the north-west of Iran was a troubled area. As has already been described, during World War II the Allies occupied Iran to secure supply routes to the Soviet Union. Great Britain occupied the south and the Soviet Union northern Iran, including the Azerbaijan region. The Soviets did not withdraw their troops after the war, as had been agreed in the Tripartite Treaty, remaining there in order to extend their influence and encouraging the secession of the areas under their control with the ultimate aim of their joining the Soviet Union.

There were two quite separate independence movements, each with its own aims, but both supported by the Soviets.

Azerbaijan province is contiguous with the borders of Turkey, Armenia and the Republic of Azerbaijan which at the time was part of the Soviet Union. As well as speaking Farsi, almost all of the inhabitants of Azerbaijan province in Iran speak Azeri, a Turkic language, and many feel closely aligned to Turkish culture. In this they are similar to the population of the Azerbaijan Republic. There was (and there remains) an independence movement whose aim was to obtain greater autonomy, if not union with the Soviet Union. At the same time there was in Iran a strong and developing Communist Party – the Tudeh party (the Hezb-e-Tudeh) – whose aim was the establishment of a communist regime and alignment with the Soviet Union, and which opportunistically adopted and supported the Azeri independence movement.

Taking advantage of the Soviet presence and political instability, local Azeri separatists and leftist groups, supported by the Soviets, rose up against the central Iranian government in late 1945, and gained control of parts of the province and established their own administration. The Azerbaijan People's Government declared an autonomous government in Iranian Azerbaijan in December 1945 under the leadership of Ja'far Pishevari, a prominent communist and nationalist figure. The ultimate aims were independence and eventually incorporation into the Azerbaijan Republic within the Soviet Union; but as a first step, and in order to gain maximum support, the People's Government sought autonomy within Iran while also promoting leftist, pro-Soviet policies.

The central Iranian government was unable to quell the insurgency immediately owing to Soviet occupation and post-war instability. However, international pressure, especially from the United States and the newly formed United Nations, forced the Soviet Union to withdraw its forces from northern Iran in May 1946 – one year after the end of the second world war and within six months of the beginning of the uprising. This seems extraordinary today in view of the imperviousness of the current Russian government to international opinion.

Once the Soviet troops withdrew, the Iranian army quickly moved to retake control of Azerbaijan Province. Shahriar, now a Captain with a company comprising five platoons of about 25 men each and each led by a lieutenant, was sent as part of a battalion to reclaim the province and clear out the insurgents. During their retreat, in December 1946, the insurgents had partly destroyed the Kiz Bridge over the Qezel Ozan River 20 km. southeast of Mianeh in Eastern Azerbaijan, in a futile attempt to halt the advance of the Imperial Army. The battalion needed to cross the river – the alternative would have required an extensive detour in order to attain Tabriz, the capital of Azerbaijan where the insurgents had established their revolutionary government. Shahriar, applying lessons he had absorbed while at the Military Academy, crossed the river carrying a rope which he secured at the other bank, so allowing others to cross, and using tree trunks and rocks from the destroyed bridge formed a pontoon that allowed the entire battalion to cross safely without a single casualty. For this he received a citation and the Sepah decoration 'for military prowess'.

In late December 1946, the Iranian forces of which Shahriar was part, entered Tabriz and swiftly dissolved the Azerbaijan People's Government just 12 months after its establishment. And by early 1947, the Iranian government had re-established control over the entire region, and most of the leaders of the separatist movement were either in flight or had been arrested.

In parallel, but separately and also fomented by the Soviet Union, was the uprising by Kurds seeking an independent Kurdistan. This was nothing new then, and the yearning for an independent homeland continues to this day. Kurds are present in some numbers in Iran, Iraq, Syria and Turkey, and their quest for an independent national home is long-standing. It is also understandable. They speak a different language from others, are ethnically different and have a strong culture, common to them all, regardless of the boundaries of the countries in which they happen to be.

In 1946, as with the Azeri separatists, and taking advantage of the weakness of the Iranian government after the Second World War and of the presence of the Soviet Union and the assistance that the Soviet Union was providing, Kurdish insurgents established a government in Mahabad and declared independence.

At first, and especially considering the presence and strength of the Soviet Union in the area – as with the Azeri insurgency – the Iranian government seemed powerless to counter these moves. However, and for the same reasons as the failure of the Azeri uprising – not least the withdrawal of Soviet support – the Kurdish adventure collapsed. The Iranian authorities quickly and relatively easily reestablished their authority, the Mahabad government was crushed and the insurgency was largely – but not entirely – pacified with little fighting.

By all accounts, though, whereas the people of Tabriz welcomed the Iranian forces and with the taking of the city the Azeri rebellion was extinguished, the Kurds in Mahabad were not so accepting of the loss of the prospect of an independent Kurdistan. While the bulk of the resistance died in Mahabad, there remained partisans who were active – not in the city itself but in the mountainous area round about

– and who were pushed further and further towards the Soviet borders. These comprised small bands of men who were irritants, but posed no significant threat to the Iranian government.

But they had to be subdued – recently one band had attacked a local army patrol, and they had also assassinated a local administrator. By early in 1947, the situation in Azerbaijan was stable and quiet. Shahriar's company was diverted from Azerbaijan to Kurdistan, and sent to an army base in Rezaieh[16] 140 km west of Tabriz and 120 km north of Mahabad the self-declared capital of Kurdistan. Once there they were tasked with eliminating these remaining insurgents.

Shahriar was happy to go. He knew and loved this area, having been stationed there at various times since he was commissioned in 1937 when there was no apparent problem, but where the potential for trouble was ever present. He was especially fond of the Kurdish people, an affection that was to prove deeply ironic. In his words the Kurds were honest, simple and generous people, and despite being Muslim were very close to his culture and community. He even learned a little of their language which, he said, was similar to the Dari language spoken by Zoroastrians.

One of the photos we have shows him in Kurdish traditional costume, taken during an earlier stay in the area, not as fancy dress but because at that time the military was attempting to win hearts and minds in the Kurdish region to stave off incipient insurgency. Soldiers were billeted among the local population and encouraged to integrate with them as far as was possible. However, the Kurds had long yearned for a homeland of their own, and do so to this day; and now he was sent to fight against them and put down a Kurdish rebellion. This was quite a different matter. This move was to be a turning point – a tragic turning point – in his life, and it is a terrible irony that it was at the hands of Kurds that he suffered his tragedy.

Shahriar's account of what happened subsequently is sketchy, not least because he had no clear recollection of the events immediately preceding the disaster that befell him – but also, it has to be said, he was reticent to talk about so traumatic and life-changing an event. However, over time and many discussions, a reasonably accurate picture has emerged.

The insurgent band had been spotted around the small town of Balanej, 25 km south of Rezaieh, and Shahriar was tasked with rooting them out. Because the insurgency was all but over and the area had been relatively quiet this was seen as a low-key threat, and so required only a low-key response. Based on intelligence reports from scouts, he located the band to a 25km square area, and allocated each of three platoons a portion of this area to patrol, returning to base camp in phases, the first after 48 hours, the second 24 hours later and so on, with a fourth held in reserve to rotate with the returning platoon. The fifth platoon was to be the HQ. He would usually have stayed in the HQ but one of the lieutenants had fallen sick with malaria – common in the area.[17] So Shahriar decided to take his place and lead his platoon – reduced to 20 men because of malaria and other conditions – during its tour of duty in the field. This suited him well. Apart from anything else, he was glad of the opportunity to get out of the camp.

Shahriar's recollection during the first day was of a forested valley in the mountain, with sunshine dappling through the leaves, occasional sightings of wild goats and punctuated with the howls of wolves. A magical place where it was difficult to imagine any harm – so different from Jafarabad, surrounded by desert and where forests and streams were only seen in books. He remembers no more, but we know how events unfolded from the only other survivor of the attack.

Having camped in a clearing overnight by the Barandouz river – a small stream swollen by the melting snow and winter rain – shortly after dawn on 15th April 1947 when the platoon, having had breakfast, was falling in and preparing to break camp, a hand grenade exploded among them, followed immediately by two others; and those were followed by a barrage of bullets. The attackers had clearly been waiting to cause as much damage as possible – and they succeeded. The platoon was taken entirely by surprise, 7 or 8 men were immediately killed and most of the remaining 20 were injured, some gravely, Shahriar among them. His face was badly damaged – it later transpired that he had lost one of his eyes immediately, blown out of his face, and the other was severed from the optic nerve. A few of the soldiers ran for their lives – a bad mistake as they were killed before they could get very far.

The scene was one of devastation – dead and severely injured soldiers scattered around the clearing, silent apart from the moans and lamentations of the injured. A band of insurgents appeared from the trees, and immediately shot dead any among the victims who showed signs of life. And then they began to strip the corpses of their valuables and weapons, Shahriar included, whose wedding ring was removed from his finger. He was fortunate – unconscious and inert, and taken for dead – otherwise he would certainly have been killed along with the others. Apart from Shahriar and one seriously injured private soldier, only one other survived and the details of the ambush have been recounted by him. Ahmad was a raw teenage conscript from Ahvaz in the South of Iran who had only joined a month or so earlier. He had had the good fortune of going into the trees to relieve himself immediately before the attack, and then had the wit to hide in the nearby forest rather than run and reveal himself to the attackers. Ahmad witnessed everything that followed the attack which proved to be the deadliest of the entire insurgency and left 17 men dead, two, including Shahriar, seriously injured and only Ahmad unscathed.

Assuming that all of his comrades were dead Ahmad stumbled back to a road, losing his way many times and on one occasion coming close to encountering the group that had slaughtered his comrades. Shahriar's platoon was due to have returned to base camp during the evening of the second day, but having failed to do so the alarm was raised, and a patrol had been dispatched from Mahabad to try to locate them and to find out what if anything had gone amiss. By good fortune, just as Ahmad reached the road, he encountered this patrol.

It was not until very early the next morning that the search party, moving cautiously lest they too should be victims of an attack, reached the place of ambush. Shahriar had by then regained consciousness – indeed, he had done so some time previously – and said that he thought that the cold of dawn had revived him. He experienced a kaleidoscope of emotions, drifting in and out of consciousness. Unbearable pain; panic about the extent of his injuries (he could not see but he did not know why, and he could barely move); fear that he would die alone in that distant and remote forest; and grief, not for himself but for Laal and their unborn child. The rescuers found him among the corpses and realised that he, and another fortunate comrade who had also been left for dead, were still alive. Shahriar, being an officer, was strapped to a donkey (his non-commissioned comrade was dragged and manhandled) and in terrible pain was taken to the road where a lorry took him first to a rudimentary field hospital located in a tent, and then to the first aid base in his barracks. But the treatment was basic, there were no antibiotics, and his face became badly infected where the shrapnel had damaged it. He was driven from Mahabad to the military hospital in Tabriz, but even there, although some treatment was provided, no effective treatment was available for his most serious injuries.

While he was in hospital in Tabriz the Shah visited him and the other wounded soldier. Shahriar was still in a state of complete shock and barely registered this first encounter with the Shah who pinned on him the Sepah decoration for military prowess for the Kiz bridge action referred to above (the medal for valour was to follow later). In pinning the medal on him, sitting or lying in his hospital bed, the Shah without realising it pierced his flesh. Shahriar, apparently, did not flinch and as soon as the Shah had left, a nurse who had seen all this removed the medal and reattached it correctly, wiping away the blood on his chest.

From Tabriz, after a few days, he was flown by military transport ordered by the Shah to Tehran and to the Sina Hospital. By the time he arrived in Tehran he was in a dreadful state. While immediate first aid had been carried out – some of the shrapnel in his body had been removed – his face had not been successfully treated, and by now it was horribly infected and swollen, especially around the eyes and particularly the eye that had been blown out.

The exact number of casualties suffered by the Iranian army during the two insurgencies is not known. From what is known, the insurgencies themselves did not result in prolonged, large-scale battles but involved a series of skirmishes, clashes, and the eventual reoccupation of the region by the Iranian military by mid-1947. So Shahriar was unfortunate to have been one of the relatively small number of victims in what was, apparently, the largest single incident suffered by the Iranian army – but not, as he sometimes mused, as unfortunate as the majority of his comrades who had accompanied him on this mission.

Laal had to be told – but not yet, he implored the hospital staff. He could not bear the thought of her seeing him in his present state, and had hopes that his sight might yet be restored. He asked for Kaikhosrow, his brother-in-law, to be called.

Laal was already becoming increasingly concerned as she had heard nothing from Shahriar recently – they had previously communicated with each other by telegram every few days – just a few words to reassure each that the other was safe and well. Her two brothers – Kaikhosrow and Mehraban – had heard that there had been some incident in Kurdistan but had not yet heard about Shahriar's involvement. However, sensing that something was amiss and in order to reassure Laal who was now heavily pregnant and due to give birth, they concocted telegrams from Shahriar in order to reassure her. But whether because of the anxiety or for other more natural reasons, and sadly, she went into premature labour and the baby was stillborn. As Claudius said in Hamlet "When sorrows come, they come not single spies but in battalions". Shortly after, Kaikhosrow and Mehraban heard that Shahriar was in hospital in Tehran, and Kaikhosrow visited him there.

Over the next few days Kaikhosrow told his sister the terrible news: she still grieving for the loss of her stillborn child. But Shahriar was adamant that he did not yet wish to see her, believing that this was for her good, but as likely because he was not yet ready to face her grief. It fell also to Kaikhosrow to tell Shahriar about the loss of his firstborn, adding to his pain but confirming his interpretation of a dream. Shortly before the ambush he dreamed that he had picked three lemons from a lemon tree: the first was bad but the two others were ripe and beautiful. He had three children, the first of whom stillborn.

Eventually, a month after his arrival in Tehran, Laal and Shahriar were united in the hospital. One can imagine the emotions that flowed between them, as they mourned the loss of their child as well as the loss of Shahriar's sight.

Shahriar arrived at the Tehran hospital in late April 1947. They did their best – they certainly assured his life and cleaned up his injuries as far as they could, removing shrapnel and other debris from his body. One thing though that they were not going to be able to do was to save his sight. As described above, one of his eyes was completely blown out and the other seriously degraded – severed from the optic nerve.

During this time he was in a hospital ward with two other soldiers who had also been injured in the hostilities – one from the Azerbaijan and the other from the Kurdistan conflicts. Shahriar's comrade who had survived the attack in Mirabad had, sadly, by now died.

In June, after Shahriar had been in hospital for two months, the hospital was visited by the young Mohamed Reza Shah – the son of

Reza Shah Pahlavi who had been deposed by the British and their allies during the war for not being sufficiently committed to their cause. Shahriar had been visited by the Shah once before in hospital in Tabriz, but he was only dimly aware of that, as he had been under heavy sedation at the time and in considerable pain. He was fully conscious now.

Mohammed Reza Shah

The Shah was clearly moved and, according to Shahriar, for a short while speechless, after touching him on the arm and taking his hand.

He told Shahriar that the country owed him an immeasurable debt of gratitude for the sacrifice that he had made. How could he repay the debt? Whatever Shahriar requested of him, he would make it his business to ensure was granted.

Shahriar was a huge admirer of the Shah – to a point that might be described as worship. He was on a pedestal above other mortals, and to have the Shah visit him and even hold his hand was beyond anything he could have dreamed. His views about the Shah were with him throughout his life, and the 1979 revolution broke his heart. After the Shah had been deposed, he would often sit in his armchair muttering about the four Satans who had brought about the Shah's downfall – "Jimmy Carter, Jim Callaghan, Helmut Schmidt and Giscard d'Estaing, may they rot in hell". He was simply rehearsing a view common in Iran and indeed in most Middle Eastern countries, that nothing happens in this world without the connivance, or even the instigation, of the United States and Great Britain (that had been a long-held view dating back to the 18th century and even before – except that the roles of the great Satan and the little Satan (the United States and United Kingdom) had in the meantime reversed).

Shahriar's reactions were of confusion, humility and deep gratitude. To be visited by the Shah was to Shahriar like being visited by a god. And yet here he was, talking to the Shah who said that he, the Shah, owed him a debt. He collected his thoughts and replied that hard though it was for him and for his family to be in his present state, he was proud to have been able to serve his Imperial Majesty and the nation which he so wisely and justly led, and that he would not have had it any other way. But there was one thing that he would ask if it should prove possible. Would it be possible to send him to a hospital in the West to see whether they would be able to save his sight?

The Shah, who had been briefed by the doctors, knew that this was very likely a hopeless request, but had no hesitation in agreeing. He said that he would arrange for the procurement of the very best medical treatment available in the world. That request, and the Shah's response, were to lead to Shahriar's life taking another and fundamental shift in direction, as will be seen in what follows. Meanwhile, there and then, at his hospital bedside, the Shah pinned on Shahriar the highest decoration and medal for valour in the Iranian military[17] – the second time he had decorated him while in hospital – and on the spot promoted him from Captain to Major (which might seem like a meaningless gesture, but one which will have impacted his pension – of which more later). It is of interest, however, that while this promotion was official and is evidenced by subsequent correspondence with the Iranian Embassy in London, which always addressed him as 'Sargord' (Major) Bekhradnia, he introduced himself to UK authorities as 'Captain', and that is how he was known officially in the UK.

Shahriar remained in hospital for a further three months, although no effective treatment was administered. But it did take a long time for his other wounds, beside his eyes, to be treated. He had received extensive shrapnel wounds throughout his body, but over time these were dealt with, and by September he was in reasonable physical health and allowed to return home.

In all this time, as may be imagined, Laal and her family visited him in his hospital bed, as did his mother Shirin who, it will be remembered, had moved from her home in Jafarabad to their home in Tehran much to the chagrin and discomfort of Laal. It had been especially difficult for her during the times when Shahriar was absent on duty away from Tehran, and Shirin ruled the roost – and Laal was too timid to object, adopting the traditional and expected role of the subservient daughter-in-law. But now that Shahriar was back in Tehran, in hospital, it was doubly difficult. Not only did she have to bear her own grief, but that of Shahriar's mother as well whose weeping and wailing from morning to night was incessant. After a while Shahriar had to ask Laal to come to the hospital secretly and avoid bringing his mother who caused disruption and upset to the other patients and staff.

He went home in September, but it was a most unhappy time, other than being united with his wife and her family. He could not bear to go out and would not receive guests, because he imagined that all he would receive from others was pity. A blind man in Iran had very little status, and he remembered Sharokh, his near neighbour in Jafarabad, blinded as a result of untreated catraracts and whose lot it was to sit in a corner all day, or outside at the back of the house, hidden from the world. He imagined his life going in a similar direction, although he at least had the hope of treatment in a western hospital.

True to his word, the Shah had set wheels in motion to have Shahriar taken to England and treated. The matter was taken up at a high level – officials from the Iranian foreign office were in touch with the British Embassy; and because of the involvement of the Shah the arrangements were put in place at a diplomatic level. But the wheels turned very slowly. From time to time Shahriar was summoned to the foreign office, and once to the British Embassy, to be supplied with the necessary papers and to be briefed about what would happen. At last a date was set – 12 December 1947.

The date approached and, as a parting gift, Laal became pregnant a month or so before he left, though the pregnancy was not even suspected by the time Shahriar left Tehran. The parting was painful and poignant. This was a newly married couple – they had been married for just two years, and in the meantime they had lost one child, he had lost his sight, they had spent barely a fraction of those two years together and they scarcely knew each other – and he was departing for a foreign land which was utterly beyond their comprehension.

The Shah's office had arranged for Shahriar to travel on a plane of the Shah's Imperial flight – a DC 3, converted from a military Dakota, which routinely transported senior officials and royalty to destinations around the world. He was to be accompanied by an escort, Firouz, a member of the Iranian Armed Forces, who had been to London himself previously; and on arrival in London he was to be handed over to a member of the embassy staff in London. The Embassy had made arrangements for his hospital treatment and care.

A DC3 – similar to the one that transported Shahriar to England

Shahriar had not slept the night before, and nor had Laal. They were well aware of what a major undertaking this journey would be and how much hung on it. Laal and Shahriar sat up much of the night talking about what the future might hold (they did not yet know that Laal was pregnant) and spoke optimistically of the possibility of a cure – though to Laal at least, looking at his face, it was obvious that no cure was likely. And then next morning Kaikhosrow, Laal's brother and Shahriar's good friend, accompanied him to the airport.

Shahriar had forbidden his wife or his mother to accompany them. He was anxious about their emotional responses, and in particular that his mother, Shirin, would create a scene which would make it all the more difficult for him, as she did regularly. So he left home with a small suitcase, stoical and upright, with wife and mother weeping without control in the street as neighbours watched the sad parting.

The journey to the airport was brief. They arrived early and completed the minimal formalities in no time. Firouz was there to greet him and Kaikhosrow left him in his care. They said their emotional farewells, and late in the morning of 12th December 1947 Shahriar boarded the aeroplane and took off for what was to become his new home on the outer fringes of Europe. He remembered nothing of the journey. His mind was a complete whirl.

PART 2: ENGLAND

Arrival and admission to hospital

Shahriar remembered nothing of the flight. It would certainly have made at least two stops on its way to London – probably Beirut or Ankara and Rome – and they might even have spent a night in Rome. The first thing that he remembered was being told that they were now approaching London, and Firouz fussing about him, ensuring he had seatbelt tied, that his seat was upright and that he was prepared for the landing. He suddenly felt alone and very vulnerable – helpless and bereft. He remembered his heart in his mouth at the approach and landing – he had only once been in an aeroplane previously, when he was transferred, newly injured, from Tabriz to Tehran, a journey whose memory was obliterated by his feelings of pain and anguish.

The approach seemed to take an age, and then the bumps as the plane landed convinced him that it had crashed. But they survived, and the plane taxied for an interminable length of time, eventually coming to a halt. The doors opened after another long wait. There were only a small number of passengers on the plane, and he must have been close to the front because as the doors opened, he remembered a blast of cold hitting him, causing him to shiver involuntarily – he said he had never shivered so violently before. He was used to cold – Tehran could be cold in winter – but the air was different. It had a damp quality that he was not used to, and it smelled different.

He had already surrendered his travel documents to Firouz on the aeroplane, who had told Shahriar to stay seated while he sorted out the formalities. So he remained alone on the plane – no one really took very much notice of his presence and he had little idea what was going on. Once again, he felt abandoned. But it was not long before Firouz came back telling him that he could now leave the plane and that the arrangements for his transport to the hospital were ready and waiting. He helped him to the door of the plane and down the steps, one step at a time, and onto the tarmac.

Suddenly it hit him that he was in England. Up to now the journey from Jafarabad to Tehran, with a detour to Bombay, was as far as his imagination could have taken him. Here he was now 5000 kilometres away. And there were people round about speaking in a language which he barely recognised. He did know a few words of English – he had learned some at secondary school, but in Military Academy they had learned French in as far as they had learned any foreign language, and of course in India he had also been exposed to English – but this was quite different from anything he had heard before.

Firouz explained to him that he was going to be looked after by Kurosh from the Iranian Embassy in London – who would act as his translator initially, and guide. Shahriar felt another light touch on his arm as Kurosh spoke in Persian. "Welcome. We will help you." The words were kind, but they carried an undercurrent of pity that made his stomach churn. He hated pity. It was a reminder of what he had lost – his independence, his dignity, and more.

There was an ambulance waiting on the tarmac to transport him to the King Edward VII Hospital for Officers in central London. Kurosh, explained to him that he would accompany him, but had to sit in the front with the driver. There were no seats in the back of the ambulance, just a bed and a seat for a nurse; and although there was no reason for Shahriar to lie down – he had been sitting upright all the way through the journey – he was told that he should lie down on the bed and be strapped in. And so that is how he made the 30-minute journey from the airport – which we now know was Northolt Airport[19] – to the hospital in Marylebone, London.

The car came to a halt, and Shahriar was helped out, his shoes meeting the cold pavement. Once again, he was struck by the quality of the air – quite different from anything he had been used to previously – damp and tinged with a metallic tang he couldn't place (very likely the residue of the smog that had affected London earlier in the month). He was guided into a building, the sound of footsteps echoing on polished floors.

His first impressions were of the hushed voices and the faint antiseptic scent that stung his nose. He imagined white walls, bright lights, and rows of beds filled with broken bodies. His own body ached at the thought.

Kurosh left him briefly to arrange the admission formalities, and he was taken to a private room, the door clicking shut behind him. The silence was deafening, broken only by the rustle of sheets as he sat on the bed. A nurse spoke to him softly, her English words meaningless but soothing. She touched his arm gently, guiding his hand to a glass of water. The gesture was kind but felt patronizing, as though he were a child who couldn't find his own way.

As the days passed, his world remained cloaked in darkness. The doctors came and went, their voices calm and clinical as they discussed his condition. He felt like a ghost, drifting through the corridors of the hospital. The nurses were kind, the staff attentive, but he longed for something more. And, unsurprisingly, he found the food bland, the tea too weak. He missed the taste of Iranian khoreshts, the sweet aroma of fresh bread baking in the clay oven.[20]

His dreams were the worst. In sleep, he saw the faces of his comrades, their expressions frozen in time. He relived the explosion, the searing pain, the frantic shouts. He woke up gasping, his hands clawing at the bandages around his eyes as though he could tear away the darkness. The nurses would rush in, their voices gentle but firm, calming him with soothing words he didn't understand.

King Edward VII hospital was one of the most prestigious in London, one of the most expensive (the NHS had not yet been established) and was well regarded for its treatment. It had been bombed during the war and had been closed since 1940, not reopening in a fully functioning state until October 1948. However, there were a number of wards that were open at the end of 1947, housing patients for diagnosis who then transferred to other hospitals if necessary, and some for non-operative treatment.

Shahriar spent just 10 days there and underwent tests and assessments to establish the extent and nature of his injuries and the best treatment. In the course of his stay he was assessed by Sir Stewart Duke-Elder who was the foremost ophthalmologist of his time and based at Moorfields Eye Hospital, one of the best – perhaps the best – ophthalmic hospital in the world. His initial assessment gave no grounds for optimism, not passed on to Shahriar, and he recommended that he should be transferred to Moorfields where more specialist assessment and treatment could take place.

Kurosh returned each day and was present during assessments, explaining to him that they were assessing not only his eyesight, but other wounds that remained mainly in his face but also in other parts of his body. But the main issue was his eyesight and, ten days after his arrival in England, again accompanied by Kurosh, he transferred to Moorfields Eye Hospital, no more than a mile or two away from King Edward VII in Marylebone.

The transfer was both unsettling and hopeful. The news of the move had come abruptly, just the day before, relayed to him by Kurosh. He had grown used to the rhythms of his days at King Edward VII Hospital – the soft rustle of the nurses' uniforms, the faint scent of disinfectant, and even the steady clink of teacups in the ward. Leaving this place, where he had begun to feel a fragile sense of security, filled him with unease.

The journey to Moorfields took place early in the morning of Tuesday 23 December 1947, just two days before Christmas. He was carefully guided into a car by a nurse and Kurosh who had become a faint but steady bridge between him and this foreign world. Kurosh attempted small talk, asking him if he had slept well and if he was comfortable, but Shahriar's answers were clipped. The truth was, he couldn't shake the sense of being a parcel, passed from one place to another, without agency or choice. The frustration of his helplessness mixed with nervous anticipation. This new hospital was said to be the best for eyes, the place where miracles might happen. But what if they didn't? What if he was leaving familiarity for nothing?

The car stopped, and Shahriar was helped out and led into the hospital. The floor beneath his feet was smooth, the air inside cooler than the halls of King Edward VII Hospital. The newness of the environment made his skin prickle with discomfort. Every sound seemed sharper here – the quick steps of doctors in the corridors, the beeping of machines, and the murmur of conversations.

He was led to a private room where two nurses were awaiting him and introduced themselves in warm but professional tones. Their voices were kind, but Shahriar struggled to hold onto their names, which sounded quite unfamiliar. His mind felt overloaded with the effort of keeping up, of adjusting to yet another unfamiliar setting. The bed was made up with crisp sheets, and there was a small table with water and what he assumed was a tray of food. One of the nurses gently placed his hand on the edge of the bed to help him orient himself, her movements practised and reassuring. Her name was Nonnie and, together with her future husband Haydn, she would stay a friend throughout their lives.

That first day was a blur of activity. Doctors and nurses came in and out. They relied on Kurosh, who by now felt like an indispensable part of Shahriar's life, to translate their questions and explanations. The sheer number of people involved in his care both reassured and overwhelmed him. These were experts, clearly invested in helping him, but the complexity of it all made his head spin.

On his second day at Moorfields, Shahriar began to absorb more of the hospital's atmosphere. The staff had a brisk efficiency that was different from the quiet solemnity of King Edward VII Hospital. Here, everything felt focused, as though every person, every machine, every movement had a single purpose: restoring and maintaining vision. Shahriar could feel the weight of expertise around him, the sense that he was in a place where his blindness was not seen as a tragedy but as a challenge to be addressed with precision and care.

That morning, a nurse guided him to a chair near one of the specialized machines they would be using for diagnostics. The whirring and clicking of the equipment were alien but oddly comforting. The doctor who explained the procedure spoke with a confidence that made

Shahriar feel both hopeful and wary. "We'll do our best to assess the condition of your optic nerves," Kurosh relayed. "This will give us a clearer idea of the treatment path."

The tests themselves were a mixture of sensations – cool air on his face, gentle pressure against his forehead, and the sound of machines that reminded him of a distant factory. When it was over, he was led back to his room, where he sat quietly for a while, trying to process the experience. The hospital felt larger and more clinical than his previous one, but the staff's kindness softened the edges.

What were Shahriar's feelings and emotions during this time? In contrast to his time in hospital in Tehran, about which he did not have much to say concerning his feelings, he recalled these in some detail, describing a mixture of helplessness and gratitude. At first, the Edward VII Hospital for Officers had seemed promising. It was a place of authority and prestige, filled with doctors who spoke in confident tones and nurses who treated him with deference. But then came the announcement: he would be transferred to Moorfields Eye Hospital for specialized treatment. He hadn't been consulted and was given less than one day's notice. He realised that the feeling of resentment that this brought on – or rather of powerlessness – was irrational, and that to be transferred to the specialist hospital was necessary. Indeed, it was what had been envisaged at the outset; and the hospital to which he was being transferred had been described to him by his brother-in-law, Kaikhosrow, as the best ophthalmic hospital in the world. But it was a feeling that he nevertheless had. The transfer made him feel powerless, like a chess piece being moved from one square to another. Yet he appreciated, nevertheless, that the decision had been made in his best interest.

So, alongside the frustration Shahriar felt a profound gratitude. The kindness of those around him often caught him off guard. The staff at both hospitals had gone out of their way to make him comfortable. They guided him with gentle hands, tried as best they could to describe every movement before making it, and answered his hesitant questions with patience, though the inevitable language barriers led to some hilarious misunderstandings – such as when he was asked if he wanted a bottle for the night and he thought he was being asked if he wanted a glass of beer (because hospitals regularly provided beer, or more commonly stout, for its "medicinal properties"!)

At King Edward VII Hospital, one of the nurses had taken the time to learn a few phrases in Persian, surprising him one morning with a carefully pronounced "Khoob khabidi?" ("Did you sleep well?"). The simple gesture had moved him deeply. Even at Moorfields, where the environment was more clinical, the staff exuded a warmth that cut through the sterility of the place. The doctors spoke with a kind of quiet confidence that gave him hope, even when their explanations felt overwhelming, the doctors describing his condition in terms that were precise but compassionate. They didn't promise miracles, but he was reassured that he was receiving the best care possible.

As the days began to unfold, Shahriar's feelings swung between frustration and gratitude. At times, the frustration reared its head, fierce and relentless. He hated relying on others for everything – for walking down a hallway, for understanding his treatment plan, for finding his way to the toilet. His independence had been stripped from him, and he couldn't see a way to reclaim it. He hated not knowing the layout of the hospital, being led from one room to another like a blindfolded child in a game. He hated the sound of people talking about him in English, their voices low and professional, as though he were an object of study rather than a person. Most of all, he hated the uncertainty – the endless waiting for results, for answers, for some sign that all of this effort would lead to something tangible.

But he also understood that the people around him were doing their best to restore what they could. So, alongside the frustration was a deep and growing gratitude. The staff at Moorfields treated him with a respect that eased his frustration. They didn't rush him, didn't make him feel like a burden. They explained things patiently, even if it took time, and they went out of their way to ensure he was comfortable.

And then there were the small moments that kept him going – the nurse who placed a cup of tea in his hands with a cheerful comment about the weather, the ward assistant who took time to teach him English words for common objects, and above all Nurse Nonnie, who befriended him, and never passed up a moment to spend time with him – chatting slowly and ensuring that he understood what she was saying. Her strong Welsh accent sometimes got in the way of communication, but the kindness was overwhelming.

These acts of kindness were like beams of light piercing the darkness. He marvelled at the lengths these strangers went to for him, a blind soldier from a distant land. They didn't have to care, yet they did. They treated him not as a burden but as a person deserving of their time and effort. This was a feeling to recur many times over the coming months. The people around him, from the surgeons to the cleaning staff, were invested in his recovery. Their efforts made him want to fight for his own future, even if that future looked so different from the one he had planned.

Although Shahriar still hated the lack of control, he began to take pride in small victories – learning to navigate his room without assistance, memorizing the names of the doctors and nurses and recognising them by their voices, managing a polite "thank you" in English when a nurse brought his meals, and even succeeding in holding brief conversations. Each accomplishment felt like a step toward reclaiming the independence he had lost. Indeed, as will be seen in what follows he made astonishing strides with his English, and became fairly proficient very quickly.

Shahriar knew the road ahead would be long and uncertain. There were no guarantees that the treatments would restore his sight, no assurances that he would return to the life he had known before the explosion. But for the first time since his injury, he felt a glimmer of hope – not just for his recovery, but for his ability to adapt.

He wasn't sure if he would ever stop feeling like a stranger in this country, but it was apparent that the people who cared for him had given him more than just medical treatment. They had given him dignity, compassion, and the courage to face the unknown. And for that, he would always be grateful.

Extraordinarily, and to our good fortune, the hospital has the detailed clinical notes of all patients, even back as far as 1947.[21] These notes reveal that Shahriar had been examined, as mentioned, by Sir Stewart Duke-Elder who was the senior consultant at Moorfields. One of his eyes was completely missing from its socket, which had itself been badly damaged; and the other could barely identify movement or distinguish between light and dark, and was useless. So saving his sight was not something that was even contemplated at present, though they did think it might be worth reviewing if anything had changed in a few months.

But in many ways, no less immediately important was that his eyes and socket still contained many fragments of the hand grenade that had caused his injury, and there was a serious risk of infection which could lead to grave consequences. Sir Stewart Duke-Elder judged that to operate immediately in order to extract the shrapnel would be unwise, and that their efforts should be focused on ensuring that infection did not occur, to which end he underwent a regime of regular penicillin injections.

So early on, and viewed objectively it was no surprise, he was going to be blind without any chance of his sight being restored. Shahriar had been in Moorfields for just a week, and it fell to the consultant surgeon under whose care Shahriar was placed – Mr Cross – to break this news to him, though it was poor Kurosh, the interpreter from the embassy, who felt the burden most acutely. He had grown attached to Shahriar over the time that he had known him, and while he knew the likely outcome from early on, it was he who had to break the news – something he dreaded.

When the doctor finally delivered the devastating confirmation, Shahriar felt the words hit him like a thunderclap. He could tell from Mr Cross' demeanour and voice that he was imparting bad news despite his calm and measured tone; but it was with Kursosh's words – hesitating and uncertain – that the message rang out with cruel clarity: there was no treatment. No surgery. No miracle. Mr Cross did offer the possibility of a review in July, but he said that it was unlikely that anything would change, and so Shahriar should reconcile himself now to blindness. The faint hope he had clung to like a lifeline during his time in England evaporated in an instant.

For a moment, the room seemed to tilt around him. Though he could not see, he could feel the weight of the doctor's presence, the gentle, regretful stillness in the air. It felt as though the world had conspired to hold its breath. Kurosh's voice faded into silence, and all Shahriar could hear was the pounding of his own heart.

Shahriar sat motionless, gripping the edge of his chair so tightly that his knuckles ached. His mouth was dry, his breathing shallow, his thoughts frozen. How could this be it? How could the journey, the pain, and the months of uncertainty culminate in nothing?

He had prepared himself for many outcomes, or so he thought. But the finality of this one – of being told he would be blind for the rest of his life – was like a door slamming shut. It was too much to process, too vast and all-encompassing to fully comprehend. He didn't speak, not immediately. What was there to say? What words could bridge the gulf between this moment and the life he had imagined for himself?

As the shock began to wear off, a flood of emotions overwhelmed him. Grief arrived first, sharp and unrelenting. It wasn't just the loss of sight – it was the loss of the future he had planned, the loss of independence, the loss of the man he had been. He thought of Laal in Iran, and of his family who had prayed for his recovery, who had placed their faith in the expertise of this foreign hospital. How would he tell them? How would he face their disappointment, their tears?

Then came anger, hot and consuming. He felt it rising in his chest like a tide, threatening to choke him. Why had he been sent here, dragged halfway across the world, only to be told there was nothing to be done? Why had no one told him sooner, sparing him the false hope, the agonizing uncertainty? But the anger had nowhere to go, and instead he kept it bottled up inside him.

Despair followed closely behind, a weight so immense it threatened to crush him. The realization that this was his life now – a life in darkness – pressed down on him with unbearable force. He thought of all the things he would never do again: see the faces of his loved ones, watch the sun rise over the Alburz mountains, walk through a crowded bazaar without fear of stumbling. The world felt infinitely smaller.

The doctor's voice broke through the haze, low and steady. Kurosh interpreted, but didn't need to. Though Shahriar couldn't understand the English, he could hear the sincerity in the tone, the effort to convey empathy. Kurosh translated softly, explaining that while there was no cure, the hospital would provide resources and support to help him adapt to his new reality. They spoke of rehabilitation, of tools and techniques that could help him navigate the world without sight.

But Shahriar barely heard these words. They felt like a poor consolation, a paltry offering in the face of such a monumental loss. He nodded stiffly, more out of politeness than agreement, his mind too clouded to process the details.

When the meeting was over, Mr Cross left but Kurosh stayed on – though there was nothing he could say or do that would help and the ensuing silence was painful. Shahriar asked him to leave. He was alone in his room. The silence felt suffocating, pressing in on him from all sides. He sat on the edge of his bed, his hands resting limply in his lap. The tears came then, hot and unchecked. He buried his face in his hands, his shoulders shaking with the force of his sobs. He cried not just for what he had lost, but for the man he used to be – the soldier who had marched off to do his duty for his Shah and country, full of purpose and certainty, and who had returned broken and blind.

The grief felt endless, a deep chasm with no bottom. He cried until there were no tears left, only a hollow ache in his chest. And then he sat in silence once more, his thoughts a jumble of regret, anger, and an aching loneliness.

These were the feelings and the scene that Shahriar was able to recount in heartbreakingly vivid detail.

The next couple of days were difficult as the reality of the future bore in. However, as time passed, the initial storm of emotion began to subside, leaving behind a strange stillness. In that quiet, Shahriar began to reflect on the kindness he had experienced since arriving in England. The nurses who had taken the time to learn and pronounce his name, the doctors who had treated him with dignity, the interpreter who had stayed late to ensure he understood every word. They hadn't been able to restore his sight, but they had given him something else: compassion, respect, and the assurance that he wasn't alone in this struggle.

These more positive feelings – or at least less negative – were reinforced on the third day after Mr Cross' interview when he was visited by Miss Goole, Chief Welfare Officer of St Dunstan's. This visit and its consequences are described in more detail in the next chapter, but suffice it to say here that the visit was positive and full of hope; and all this positivity helped Shahriar to realise that his life wasn't over, even if it felt that way now. He didn't know how he would move forward, but he knew he had to try. The alternative – giving up entirely – was not an option. He thought of his family, of their unwavering love and belief in him, and he resolved to find a way to live for them, if not for himself.

That night, as Shahriar lay in bed, he felt a fragile sense of resolve beginning to take root. The grief and anger were still there, raw and unyielding, but beneath them was a flicker of determination. He didn't know what the future held, but he knew he wouldn't face it alone. The hospital had promised to help him adapt, and for now, that was enough. It was a small step, but it was a step nonetheless.

He closed his eyes – not that it made a difference – and let the quiet of the room envelop him. For the first time since the doctor's words, he allowed himself to imagine a life beyond the darkness. It was a faint and uncertain vision, but it was there, waiting to be discovered. And Shahriar, though broken, would find a way to see it.

Shahriar was discharged from Moorfields on 22 January 1948, and went straight to the St Dunstan's facility at Ovingdean, described below. His discharge took place exactly one month less one day after his admission. During this month the doctors strove to eliminate the risk of infection and mapped a treatment plan. No immediate surgery was thought possible, but they decided that he should return in 6 months for further assessment and possible treatment.

Shahriar's second stay at Moorfields was less dramatic than the first. He was readmitted on 27 July 1948, this time for just under a month, and was discharged on 21 August. During this month the doctors were able to resume the treatment that they thought it too risky to address on his first visit – the risk of infection had largely passed and his condition was stable. There remained numerous fragments in his eye, sockets and face, but they were able to take advantage of a revolutionary new form of treatment to extract many of these without the need for aggressive operations. The giant Haab magnet was a newly developed electromagnetic device, which they used to extract those fragments that were nearest the surface. This meant that only the deeper embedded metal would need to be removed by the operations which followed later. They also made one last attempt to restore some sight to his right eye, but it was hopeless – he had by then even lost the ability to distinguish between light and dark.

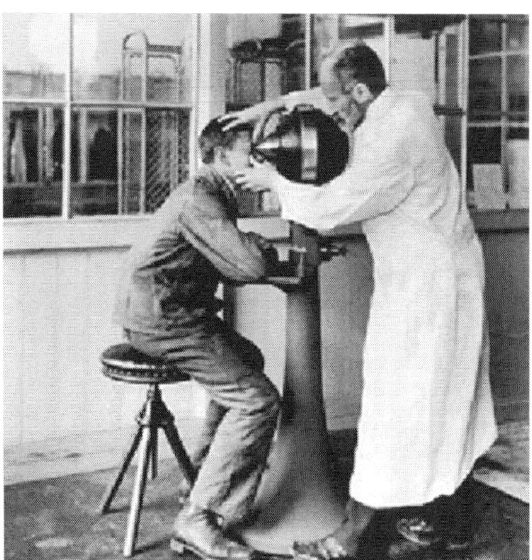

Haab magnet at Moorfields Eye Hospital

With his discharge they said that they had done all that they could, and that his face and eyes were now stable – there was no need for him to return. And indeed his face had been largely healed, and apart from his eyes, one of which was completely missing and the other of which had no colour – it was and remained a milky colour throughout his life – his face had returned more or less to its former handsome self. He had been furnished with a glass eye to put in the empty socket, but the effect of a staring unseeing eye was worse than having no eye at all, and although he did wear his glass eye from time to time, at home he generally did not, and when he went out he wore dark glasses, which made him look rather distinguished.

It was during this second stay at Moorfields that Shahriar made firm friends with Nonnie the nurse, who was by now engaged to Haydn – now working in a department store in London, but originally from Ebbw Vale, which is where Nonnie came from. They stayed close friends throughout their lives, Nonnie and Haydn often visiting our family. On one occasion – before Laal and Bahram had arrived in England – Shahriar visited them in Ebbw Vale (presumably he took a tortuous train journey to get there), and recounts how he had a bath in a tin tub in front of the fire! Laal was ambivalent about her husband having done such a thing with a young woman she had never met.

St Dunstan's

In the day or two following Mr Cross' prognosis – something he had feared and anticipated but which nevertheless came as a shattering blow – he drifted between determination to make the best that he could of his life, and a haze of despair, though in truth the despair predominated. The nurses were kind, the doctors professional, but there was little they could offer to assuage the deep void inside him. Shahriar contemplated life in Iran as a blind man – where he would be pitied, but could not hold a valued place in society. But what alternative was there? He had no prospect of remaining in England, far from home, with limited English and no clear path forward, and with no means of supporting himself or his family. What was to become of him? Was he bound to return to Iran? What options did he have?

There was a more immediate issue that had not even crossed Shahriar's mind previously. The treatment that he was receiving was expensive, but there was no question – it was being met by the Iranian government – and there was a hint from Kurosh that it was being met by the Shah personally. However, there was to be a second stay in hospital in 6 months – again there was no question about the payment for that. But where was he to live in the meantime? Was he to return to Iran between hospital visits? If not, what arrangements could be made for him?

The turning point came on a grey, damp afternoon, three days after the news that had left him shattered. Shahriar was sitting by the window, listening listlessly to the indistinct sounds of London traffic, when he heard a soft knock at his door. The visitor introduced herself as Miss Goole, the chief welfare officer from St. Dunstan's, an organization he had never heard of, accompanied by the ever loyal and concerned Kurosh.

Miss Goole explained that she had been informed of his situation – though how, or by whom, remained a mystery. All he heard from Kurosh was that he had been contacted by Miss Goole who had been given his contact details by the hospital. St. Dunstan's, she said, was a charitable organization founded during World War I to assist blind British and Commonwealth servicemen. "It's unusual," she admitted, "for us to take someone outside our usual remit. But we believe we may be able to help."

Shahriar listened as Miss Goole described the philosophy of St. Dunstan's: not pity, but empowerment. Their goal was to equip blind veterans with the skills and confidence to live full, independent lives. "We can't restore your sight," she said, her voice calm but resolute, "but we can help you find your way forward."

She made no specific suggestions, but chatted and said that if there was anything that he needed of a practical nature then he should get in touch through Kurosh or the hospital, and she would see what she could do.

But already, by the end of their conversation, she had clearly decided that she would do much more. Shahriar was to be welcomed into the St Dunstan's family. Miss Goole returned just two days later with a proposal, which once again Kurosh was on hand to translate. St Dunstan's would admit Shahriar as a member with all the benefits available to other members which, most immediately relevant, meant that on discharge from the hospital they would provide him with accommodation at the St Dunstan's residential centre.

What Shahriar did not know was that Miss Goole's visit had been preceded by two days of intensive discussion between St Dunstan's and the Iranian embassy – which itself no doubt had to communicate with Tehran – who agreed that they would meet all costs of Shahriar's stay at St Dunstan's and any associated costs of travel, training et cetera. The instructions from Tehran were clear: it was the Shah's wish that Shahriar should be afforded all the help they could give. And indeed, when the Shah paid a state visit to England later that year, there was a tentative plan that he would visit Shahriar. That visit

– inevitably – got crowded out, but the St Dunstan's records show that Shahriar was visited by the Shah's Aide-de-Camp and the Military Attaché – who said that they had reported back to the Shah about Shahriar's condition.[22]

This arrangement remained in place for about a year, until sometime in 1949, when Shahriar fell victim to geo-political disputes. The Anglo Iranian Oil Company, British owned, had exclusive rights to Iranian oil, as it had had since the beginning of the century, but under a new nationalist government in Iran this was about to change. There were tensions already at the end of the 1940s, and they culminated in March 1951 with the Iranian nationalisation of the company. Despite the complicated relations that developed between the United Kingdom and Iran, the Iranian embassy remained conscious of Shahriar's presence in England and from time to time would invite him to a reception or other function.

Laal and Shahriar greeted by the Iranian Ambassador and his wife

One of the consequences of the soured relations arising from what is now called the crisis in Anglo Iranian relations was that the Iranian embassy ceased reimbursing St Dunstan's for its services.

One other consequence of this diplomatic stand-off was that the Iranian government introduced strict exchange controls which meant that Shahriar's pension in Iran was frozen – it was still paid but could not be transferred to the UK. Although this caused immediate problems for Shahriar it had a silver lining which eventually became apparent. In November 1952 the St Dunstan's welfare officer stated in her periodic report that Shahriar estimated that he had £2000 in frozen salary locked up in Iran. If that was the case in 1952, then by the time the money was released in the early 1960s it would have amounted to a substantial sum of money. Although we do not know how much, it was sufficient to enable him to buy a house to let in Chiswick which supplemented his then meagre income – at that time, effectively, just his unemployment pay.

Miss Goole's message that St Dunstan's would admit him as a member, with all the benefits that were due to its members, was difficult to absorb, and he had to ask Kurosh to repeat it. Shahriar could scarcely believe what he was hearing. As mentioned, he was full of anxiety about what was to become of him on release from the hospital, and the immediate future at least now seemed to be secured. He was overwhelmed with gratitude. That somebody that he barely knew, and in a land far distant from his own, would treat him with such kindness and consideration was beyond his comprehension.

But why? St Dunstan's was founded explicitly to help British and Commonwealth servicemen. Why would the organisation adopt someone from a far distant land who had no ties with Britain? A clue is provided in a letter[23] that Miss Goole wrote to Shahriar as she was retiring a few years later. In it she said

> *I remember so well coming to see you in Moorfields in January 1948, soon after your eyes were first damaged. I was full of admiration for the wonderful spirit you showed in this bitter blow to*

> *your ambition; you were so brave, and so patient, and so sensible, all alone in a foreign land. I felt very proud to know you, and very glad that St Dunstan's could help you.*

And this seems to have been a common feature in people who encountered him. His resilience, his optimism and his realism, his humility and his determination, his honesty and his intelligence impressed and moved people – from the Shah to Kurosh to Miss Goole and to the hospital staff. It is notable reading through correspondence from the time, how even Lord and Lady Fraser – the then chairman of St Dunstan's and his wife – went out of their way to provide help and assistance to Shahriar and his family in small matters and large.[24]

Following Miss Goole's visit there were a number of others from different branches of St Dunstan's, and the first of the index cards concerning Shahriar in the St Dunstan's archive – author unknown and undated, but assumed to have been created soon after his adoption by St Dunstan's – gives his personal details, medical history and so on. It ends with the following:

> *Rapidly learning to speak English, well educated, pleasant and easy to get on with. Good type. Iranian government anxious to pay for anything that will help him.*

The term "good type" carries with it certain connotations among the British officer class and Shahriar would have been most amused, and probably a little chuffed, to know that he was considered a "good type"!

Incidentally, observations about Shahriar's intelligence were something that were a common feature throughout his life, beginning with his being picked out at the Jafarabad village school. A later St Dunstan's index card, in December 1948, one year after his arrival in the UK, remarks "has had a preliminary telephony test. Very keen and intelligent and English good".

Crucially, for Shahriar, St Dunstan's had a huge residential centre in Ovingdean, just outside Brighton with bedrooms, workshops, classrooms and recreation facilities. The photo below gives an idea of the centre, perched on the Sussex clifftop, and overlooking the sea.

The centre was intended to house members who were undergoing training or who needed a convalescent home, but it was to provide a permanent home for Shahriar for nearly two years. The St Dunstan's officer list for 1949 lists nearly 200 officers, but only Shahriar and one other had St Dunstan's Ovingdean as their home address. Shahriar was to remain at Ovingdean until December 1949.

From the moment Shahriar stepped into the sprawling Ovingdean centre, he was enveloped by an atmosphere of optimism. He was greeted warmly by the staff, who spoke to him not with pity but with respect and assurance[25] , and by fellow residents – almost all veterans from the 2nd World war – who offered camaraderie and shared stories of triumph over adversity. For the first time in months, he felt less alone.

St Dunstan's training had two key functions. The first was to help its members adapt to blindness – to show them that life continued, and could continue well, despite the lack of sight. Many of these newly blinded soldiers came to St Dunstan's in a state of despair and

St Dunstan's Centre, Ovingdean

conviction that any meaningful life was now over. So the first task was to show them that this was not so and to enable them to adapt to living as close to normal a life as possible though without vision.

So, for example, new arrivals were introduced to orientation and mobility training. Shahriar was taught to use a long cane to navigate unfamiliar environments[26]. He was also taught daily living skills, from preparing simple meals to organizing his belongings, ensuring he could live independently. One thing that he had already had to learn on arrival at the hospital was how to clean himself after going to the toilet. This is difficult enough for a blind man, but doubly difficult for somebody who has never used toilet paper before. In Iran, as in most of the rest of the world, the way of doing this is to use water and if toilet paper is to be used, it is to dry oneself. This is just a small example of the many changes of behaviour that Shahriar had to learn and accustom himself to.

Almost as important, in Shahriar's case, was the challenge of bridging the language gap. Though Shahriar's English had come on leaps and bounds since he had arrived in England just less than two months earlier, he struggled to express himself with any degree of fluency. This is where a long-time volunteer – Bertha MacAndrew, or 'Miss MacAndrew' as she was known to Shahriar and to his family – came into Shahriar's life. There were many volunteers, providing all manner of assistance, their help and activities ranging from escorting the men on walks for exercise to some very specialist activities like vocational training and placement.

On any day at Ovingdean there would be more than a dozen volunteers providing one form of assistance or another to St Dunstaners. None was more important to Shahriar than Miss MacAndrew, one of St Dunstan's longest serving volunteers, who had first offered her services during the First World War when she lived in London, soon after St Dunstan's had been established. Having moved to within 6 miles of Brighton, and following the sad influx of new members during the Second World War, she renewed her volunteering in the mid-1940s, and became a mainstay of the Ovingdean centre. She was of independent means, coming from a relatively wealthy family, and had remained unmarried. By the time she encountered Shahriar in 1948 she was already 70.

She had in the meantime taken the trouble to learn Braille, in order to be able to teach it to new St Dunstaners, but initially she undertook to help Shahriar improve his English[27]. Her devotion was remarkable. Scarcely a day went by without her spending time with him, helping him with his English, taking him for walks on the sea front, and helping him adjust to his blindness. As with so many others, she was deeply impressed with the man, and was shortly to show him and his family singular generosity and kindness.

Improving his English language skills was the first task, but remarkably quickly he had developed this sufficiently to begin to learn Braille, something which Miss MacAndrew was also able to teach him. He found this difficult but his fingers gradually became accustomed to deciphering the raised dots that would provide him with access to books and newspapers. The process was slow, often frustrating, but Miss MacAndrew's patience and encouragement kept him going. Indeed, extraordinarily, by July 1948 he had progressed sufficiently to pass the National Institute for the Blind[28] proficiency test in reading Braille, and by October of the same year he passed the proficiency test for writing Braille. We know this because on each occasion he received a letter from Lord Fraser – the Chairman of St Dunstan's – congratulating him and sending him a £1 note in recognition of his achievement!

In December 1948 he received an invitation from the recently created UNESCO to attend a meeting in Paris of an international committee attempting to standardise Braille across different languages and scripts. We do not know how he came to be invited to that meeting, but imagine that the Persian government may have suggested him or that the invitation came via a Professor Darab – an Iranian professor at SOAS who, it seems, may have had knowledge of Braille and who also attended the meeting. Shahriar went, but we do not know what part if any he played in the discussion.

There was a follow-up meeting in April the next year from which Shahriar excused himself, and when the conclusions of the meetings were circulated, he replied saying that it was all too difficult for him and that he had no comment to offer. That really isn't surprising. The attachment to the letter on which he was invited to comment would have been difficult even for a sighted expert and included pages and pages of notations in different languages and the Braille equivalents. That was the first and last time that Shahriar found himself on an international stage.

Shahriar also learned to type – another transformative life skill that enabled blind men and women to maintain contact with the sighted world. There was of course no alternative to touch typing, and Shahriar in fact became a fast and reasonably proficient typist – though his typing was inevitably littered with typing errors.

Typing proved to be an essential skill for Shahriar, enabling him to communicate with Laal. With no one in Ovingdean able to read Farsi, Shahriar used to type letters to her but using English letters to transliterate words into Farsi, and she replied similarly. It didn't always work, but it generally did; and he later acquired a Farsi typewriter, which he taught himself to use. Indeed, he not only acquired it, but he developed it and the Imperial Typewriter Company produced two prototypes, one of which was the one he used. However he failed in his attempt to persuade them to mass produce it and give him sole agency rights in Iran.

Having learned to type, and having been given a standard keyboard (standard, but with the braille letters superimposed on the keys), although a fairly proficient typist Shahriar became very frustrated about one thing. Whereas all typewriters rang a bell when the carriage reached the end of the line and needed to be moved onto the next, there was no such warning or mechanism when the end of the page was reached. So he found that very often he would be typing away, but there was no paper on which he was typing.

He spent ages thinking about this problem and how it could be resolved, and he eventually hit upon a mechanism – not complicated at all but too complicated to describe in detail here – which involved a lever and a groove. A groove was inserted into the carriage and the lever mechanism was kept out of the groove by the paper as long as there was paper in the carriage. But when the paper was out, the lever was activated into the groove and the carriage was locked.

He even had a prototype of his invention created which he used himself. And for a while St Dunstan's, the Royal National Institute for the Blind and the Olympia and other typewriter companies expressed interest in exploiting this. There are at least 30 or 40 letters on file, including an attempt at a patent application. The patent was refused because a not dissimilar patent had been sought in the States (though never in the end taken up) and in any case the typewriter manufacturers thought that it was too niche an adjustment – and that there were not sufficient blind people who would make it worth their while adopting. It was disappointing for Shahriar, but it was an example of how lively and wide-ranging his mind was.

Among the leisure activities that were available at St Dunstan's was training in crafts. At home we had a number of Shahriar's creations in plastic – bedside lights, napkin holders, rugs, bedspreads and string bags. Members were also taught how to shoot, with bow and arrow and also with rifles. They were able to make use of somewhat primitive, but nevertheless effective, auditory systems to enable participants to shoot at targets. Shahriar was a good shot, both with bow and arrow and with rifle, and we have a photo of him having captained the winning side in a shooting competition.

Shahriar's time at St Dunstan's was interrupted in July 1948 by a second spell at Moorfields Eye Hospital, already discussed above. The time he had already spent at St Dunstan's had persuaded him that life for a blind man in England was infinitely preferable to that of a blind man in Iran. He made up his mind that he would remain in England if that were at all possible, bitterly aware of what this might mean for Laal and his soon-to-be born child, but also for himself.

Bahram was born on 13 August 1948 in Tehran, while Shahriar was undergoing operations and other treatment at Moorfields. Two days later Nonnie gave him the news that a telegram had been sent by Kaikhosrow giving him the news that he had a son. This should have been a source of great joy, but the joy was mitigated by his anxiety over his future.

As has already been remarked, he had a horror of returning to Iran blind, where he saw no possible positive future. But he was torn. He had a young wife and now a son in Iran. Could he stay in England and leave them in Iran? He certainly could not insist that they come to join him in England, and leave behind their extended family and the life that they knew. But he knew a decision was needed. It broke his heart, but he had made his choice and so with the help of Kurosh he wrote to Laal shortly before his discharge for the second time from Moorfields. We do not have a copy of the letter, but we know its contents from both Laal and Shahriar himself, and also from the woman[29] to whom Shahriar gave the letter and who took it to Iran to give to Laal, and the letter below reproduces it as faithfully as we are able – certainly its sentiments are as relayed to us.

My Dearest Laal

I hope this letter finds you well, though I cannot imagine the weight you must carry.
The news of our son Bahram's birth has been the source of great joy to me, but makes this letter all the harder to write. I write this not in bitterness or regret, but in acceptance of what has happened. Life, in its cruel twist, has taken me down a path I never foresaw, and though I cannot see the world with my eyes any longer, my heart sees clearly what I must say.
The accident has left me changed in ways beyond the loss of my sight. I find myself in a land far from you, a place I did not intend to be, but now realize I may never leave. I no longer expect to return home. It may be difficult for others to understand but it is clear to me that there is some prospect of a meaningful life for a man without sight in England, which I fear is not the case in Iran. The journey ahead for me is uncertain, and as I stand on the edge

of this new, dark reality, I must face the truth. You and our son Bahram whom I must bitterly accept I will never see, deserve a life free from the burden I would bring.

Even in the short time that we have been together, you have been the light in my life, brighter than any sun, and I know that your strength, your faith in Ahura Mazda, and the wisdom of Kaikhosrow, will guide Bahram toward the man he is meant to be. But I cannot ask you to wait for a husband who may never come home, who will never be the man you married. You deserve happiness, and so does he.

With this letter, I release you from any promise, any vow made under different skies. You are free to walk your own path, to live, to love, to find joy in the days ahead without the weight of my fate hanging over you. Please, do not feel guilt or obligation – I ask this not from sadness, but because I want you both to flourish, without the shadow of my absence darkening your days.

Tell our son I love him, that my greatest sorrow is not to be able to see his face as he grows. Yet I know that in your care, he will become someone strong and kind, someone who will carry forward the light that I can no longer see. Someone who will make us both proud.

I will always hold you in my heart, even if my eyes can no longer take in the sight of you. Be well, Laal, my love. I set you free.

Yours forever, your husband,

Shahriar

This was the last time Shahriar and Kurosh met. Kurosh was based in London and Shahriar now in Ovingdean. In any case Kurosh's tour of duty in London was coming to an end and he would be returning soon to Iran. He had grown immensely fond of Shahriar and their parting was emotional and final. He was sobbing as he said that he would never forget Shahriar and how fitting it was, and indicative of the man, that his final service to Shahriar was to help write such a brave and selfless letter.

The letter was entrusted to Laal's friend Miss Firouzgar and delivered to Laal in Tehran two weeks later – soon after Shahriar had left Moorfields for the second time to return to St Dunstan's in Ovingdean.

Laal did not reply immediately. She did not need time to make a decision but rather to go through the motions of consulting her family. The view was unanimous. It was hard but she would join Shahriar in England. They would make a new life together which would be so different from the one that had been anticipated just three years previously when they married. But England was at that time regarded as one of the world's greatest countries; and they were sure that it would work out, sad though it would be to be so remote from her family and friends.

So Laal wrote to Shahriar telling him that of course she would come as soon as he told her that the time was right to do so. She wrote the letter in Farsi and Kaikhosrow did his best to transliterate it into

Laal (right) in Teheran with Bahram, sister Homayoun holding her daughter Mahvash, born 5 days after Bahram, and their younger brother Mehraban

Roman script so that it could be read in English. They sent the letter to Moorfields, which Shahriar of course by the time it was received had left, and so it took longer than it should to reach him in Ovingdean. By the time it was received he was in a state of some anxiety. His emotions were supercharged when he received the letter and it was read to him. He was relieved, elated, but doubly anxious because his future – because what he made of his life now, and he knew it would be hard – would affect the lives of others.

One of the services that St Dunstan's provided for their members was to train them for employment, and then help them find work. The list of officer members from 1949 reveals a wide range of jobs that St Dunstaners – certainly among the officers – undertook. The list includes lawyers, physiotherapists, market gardeners, and many more. The handbook that each member received included a list of professions for which St Dunstan's routinely provided training, but it also said that if there were others that were not routinely provided, it would nevertheless help arrange the training as needed.

We have not seen a list of jobs done by the non-commissioned soldiers, and perhaps that will have been quite different (there are, for example, no piano tuners among the officer class). Shahriar was not considered suitable for professional work – understandably, given that his education had been completely different, and that his English, although substantially improved and improving, would have been a barrier.

The St Dunstan's employment staff's immediate thought, with which Shahriar concurred initially, was that he should be trained as a welfare officer, to help support blind people in Iran. This was a live prospect for a while, but the thought of returning to Iran was anathema to him, and those plans were quickly abandoned, in favour of training as a telephonist. He also heard from the Iranian embassy early in 1949 that approval had been given for him to remain in the UK, and that his salary and pension would be reviewed regularly. However, it remained impossible, because of exchange controls, to transmit the salary to England.

So, his chosen occupation was to be a telephonist – operating one of the large telephone exchanges increasingly in use at that time in offices and factories. That is what he was trained to do, and that is the work that he eventually did for 10 years.

The St Dunstan's July 1949 officer roll listed Shahriar as "in training": almost certainly this will have included his job specific training as a telephonist. But beyond the training, among the services the Charity provided was job placement as well. St Dunstan's employed a dedicated team who not only found employment for members, but who supported them throughout their working lives while in employment. St Dunstan's truly was and remains a rare organisation, providing extraordinary benefits and service to its members[30]. And at the same time, the placement team was certainly assisted in its work by the fact that the UK had on the statute book the Disabled Persons (Employment) Act 1944 which required employers with 20 or more employees to ensure that at least 3% of their workforce were registered disabled persons.

Shahriar in 1949, aged 33

Despite its intentions – and indeed, despite the letter of the law – the system did not work as well as might have been hoped. The St Dunstan's archives record that the placement team made 53 applications for jobs on Shahriar's behalf before he was finally offered employment

He did not begin his telephone training until the end of January 1949, but according to the St Dunstan's records, he made good and reasonably rapid progress, and was fully competent by December of that year, having been given specific training on the important numbers at Alltools, the company where he obtained employment.

And, while he was hard at work learning to live as a blind man, improving his English, and learning the other skills which St Dunstaners acquired, St Dunstan's lobbied on his behalf and obtained permission from the Home Office and the Labour Department for him to begin working in England – so the way was clear then for him to begin work.

Shahriar was making great progress. He was, of course, always aware of his blindness, which could not but cast a pall over his life, and from time to time drove him to depression. But that never lasted long, as he reminded himself of his relatively good fortune. How much worse his life could have been but for the kindness of so many strangers. But the question remained, what was to become of him in the medium to long term?

He wanted to stay in England and he wanted his wife and son to join him – and to his great joy he had received the letter from Laal saying that that was what she too wanted. But he could not remain indefinitely at St Dunstan's, and there was no possibility of his family joining him so long as he had no income and nowhere else to live. He needed to work to earn – and with the training and job placement that was in hand; and he also needed accommodation. This is where he experienced the single act of kindness and generosity that outshone all the other many acts of kindness he had and was yet to experience – something quite unimaginable.

Miss MacAndrew had been visiting and helping Shahriar with his English, his braille and generally assisting him with his daily life and to adjust to life in England ever since he first entered St Dunstan's in January 1948. Now, 18 months later, in September 1949, after Shahriar had heard from Laal that she would join him as soon as the time was right, Miss MacAndrew discussed with him how this could be achieved. Then out of the blue one day she announced that Miss Goole (the Chief Welfare Officer) was planning to visit him that afternoon, and that she, Miss MacAndrew, would accompany her. Shahriar was mystified, and anxious.

Miss MacAndrew led Shahriar into one of the training rooms, where Miss Goole was waiting. After pleasantries that included her congratulations on the news that his wife and son might be joining him if he was able to stay in England, she said that she had some good news which would make that all more likely. Miss MacAndrew had agreed to donate a sum of money[31] to St Dunstan's, sufficient to enable them to buy a house which under the terms of the agreement Shahriar and his family might occupy rent free for as long as they required it. She had to repeat the message as it didn't sink in first time. When finally it did, Shahriar said nothing, but burst into tears. He was simultaneously assaulted by his different emotions. A load had been removed from his mind – his future in England was all but assured, and the way was clear for his wife and son to join him. But at the same time he was moved beyond measure by the unimaginable generosity of Miss MacAndrew – who owed him nothing, and who had already done him great service.

At the sight of Shahriar in tears, the poor Misses MacAndrew and Goole were also moved to tears and anyone who happened to witness the scene would have seen two middle aged ladies and one young man sitting around a table crying. The moment passed, Shahriar collected himself and made a little speech of thanks to Miss MacAndrew, to Miss Goole, to St Dunstan's and to the great country that England was, that had opened its doors to him and was helping to assuage his misfortune.

We don't know what happened next, but we imagine that they had a cup of tea[32] together and went their various ways. But before doing so, Miss Goole explained that nothing could be done until Shahriar knew where he would be working – so that the accommodation could be found near his place of work – but that she understood that his vocational training was coming on well, and that the placement team would soon get to work to find him employment: the fact that he was open as to where he worked would greatly ease their task.

And so it proved. Shortly after that, in November of 1949, Shahriar obtained employment as a switchboard operator at Alltools[33] airframes factory in Brentford, Middlesex, which he began on 30th December 1949, initially at a salary of £5/10s (£5.50) per week[34] (which had increased to £6 plus annual bonus by February 1952, and £7 per week by June 1953). Presumably the wage kept rising, and Shahin remembers opening his pay packet sometime during the 1950s and finding that his pay was £10 per week by then.

The work went well. The switchboard he had to operate was identical to the one he had been trained on at St Dunstan's, and he stayed at Alltools for 10 years until the factory closed at the end of 1959.

To our great regret in preparing this biography, we have been able to find out very little about Miss MacAndrew. We know that she was born in 1878 and died in 1962, and of course we know of her good works at St Dunstan's and her incredible generosity. And we do know also that Shahriar kept in touch with her. This photograph[35] of

Miss MacAndrew with Shahriar and Bahram – probably about 1957

Shahriar, Bahram and Miss MacAndrew, was probably taken around 1956 in Dunstable where she lived. But we know nothing more about her and nor do either Shahin or Bahram remember seeing her other than on that one occasion, though that is not of course to say that there were not other occasions that they do not remember.

Laal's arrival

Shahriar was due to start work at Alltools on 30 December 1949, and with typical generosity St Dunstan's not only found lodgings but also paid his rent – and continued to do so until he was able to move into the permanent accommodation that was provided through Miss MacAndrew's donation. So he moved into lodgings at 132 Wellesley Road, Chiswick on 27 December 1949, just a few days before his first day at work – enough time to begin orienting himself to his new surroundings. It was just a few stops on the direct 657 trolleybus from Chiswick High Road to Commerce Road in Brentford, where the Alltools factory was. The proprietors were no strangers to St Dunstan's members and understood the support that a blind lodger would need: and we know that St Dunstan's made arrangements for someone from the guest house to accompany Shahriar to and from the bus stop and get him on and off the bus; and at the other end someone from the factory to meet him.

However, this was no more than a temporary arrangement. With Laal and their young son Bahram due to join him in the near future, the single bed-sitting room was far from sufficient for a family. The Surveyor's Department at St Dunstan's had already begun the search for a suitable house to buy for their long-term use in the West London area, and at the end of February, once it was clear that Shahriar had settled well into his new job at Alltools, they identified a double bed-sitting room at Mr. Watt's boarding house on Lampton Road in Hounslow where they could live until their permanent home became available. It was sparse – a room just big enough for a double bed, a child's cot, and a small table – but it would do for now. There were no cooking facilities; Laal would later recall how she heated Bahram's milk in a small pan balanced on the back of a hot iron, and how they felt obliged to go out into the night and walk the streets to calm Bahram if he began to cry – out of fear that he would disturb the neighbours and that Mr Watt would evict them. It was far from ideal, but it was temporary, and hope lay in the future.

The date was set for 28 April 1950. Laal and Bahram would fly to England to join Shahriar, accompanied by Laal's older brother Kaikhosrow – Shahriar's old friend – who had offered to help Laal on her journey and through her first days in England. In anticipation of their arrival, Shahriar had already moved into Mr. Watt's boarding house in February. As before, arrangements were made for someone to accompany him to the bus stop each day and meet him when he returned from work. Yet not everything went smoothly.

One wet and blustery early April afternoon, Shahriar was helped off the bus as usual after work, but no one from Mr. Watt's establishment was there to meet him. The woman who normally walked him home was in bed sick, and no replacement had been arranged. For twenty long minutes, he stood there – blind and soaked in the rain – until a kind stranger noticed his plight and offered to walk him home. It was a humbling moment, a reminder of the precariousness of his independence and how reliant he remained on the kindness of others.

As the day of Laal's arrival drew closer, Shahriar was increasingly apprehensive – as no doubt was Laal as well. They were starting over – not just their life together, but in a foreign land, under very different circumstances. Gone was the comfort and security of their extended family in Tehran. In England, Shahriar earned £5/10s[36] a week at Alltools, with St Dunstan's generously covering the £5 weekly rent. This was not a lot (even if the family's effective income is taken as £10/10s per week, that equates to only about £24,000 per year in 2025 – less than two thirds of the purchasing power of the average wage in 2025). It was enough to live modestly but a far cry from the life they had once known, where Shahriar's officer's salary and Laal's work as a midwife had provided a comfortable existence. But nevertheless, his overwhelming feeling was excitement, albeit tinged with anxiety.

On the morning of 28 April, Shahriar was accompanied to Heathrow Airport by Nonnie, the nurse from Moorfields who had remained one of his most steadfast friends. Nonnie was a remarkable woman – devout, kind, and tireless in her support of Shahriar. Perhaps her Welsh Methodist upbringing played a role in her unflagging generosity, but it was clear that her friendship was motivated by genuine admiration and affection.

The day itself was cold and uninviting. Heavy snow had blanketed the southeast of England over the previous two days – an unusual occurrence for late April and a reinforcement of Shahriar's belief repeated regularly to his children and acquired while at Ovingdean from someone quoting T.S. Eliot, that "April is the cruellest month." The flight, delayed by an hour, finally arrived from Rome, completing the final leg of its long journey from Tehran.

Nonnie scanned the passengers disembarking onto the tarmac and said quietly to Shahriar, "There's a beautiful lady with a little boy in baggy shorts, and they're with a tall, dark man. That must be them." And it was.

In those days, passport and immigration controls were far less stringent, and Nonnie and Shahriar were able to greet them almost immediately. Their reunion was stilted rather than joyous. They hugged, but it was awkward. Little Bahram, overwhelmed by the strange environment and the unfamiliar figure before him, hid behind his mother's skirts, crying when introduced to the man he was told was his father.

Paying for the flight had not been as problematic as might be thought. They used some of Shahriar's accumulated salary and pension building up in Iran to meet these expenses. So they were able to pay for the tickets reasonably comfortably.

Kaikhosrow stayed in England for only a few days. He had come to help his sister through the journey and transition, to see his old friend, and perhaps to reassure himself that all was well. He lodged in his own room at Mr. Watt's boarding house – the cost of which was undoubtedly a factor in his short stay.

For Shahriar and Laal, life together in England began under trying circumstances. They were strangers once more, both to each other in some ways and to the country they now called home. Their living situation was cramped and uncomfortable, and cultural differences presented constant challenges.

The very first night was a case in point. The lights in their room suddenly went out, plunging them into darkness. Neither of them understood why. Laal aroused Kaikhosrow and together they went downstairs to find Mr. Watt, who explained – slowly and with some exasperation – that the electricity was powered by a coin-fed meter. While he had put coins in before their arrival, it was now up to them to keep the meter fed. For Laal and Shahriar, it was yet another reminder of how far they had travelled – not just geographically, but socially and economically.

Family life

In June 1950, news came that marked the beginning of a new chapter in Shahriar and Laal's life together. The St. Dunstan's surveyor announced that he had identified a house that would be suitable for the family – a brand-new build on a site in Chiswick where a house had once stood before being obliterated by a V-bomb in the final days of the war.

Their home at 35 Thornton Avenue, Chiswick, was to be a maisonette spread over the first and second floors of a modest three-storey building, with three bedrooms – a home that would be theirs, rent-free. They occupied the house rent-free as intended by Miss MacAndrew, but in1953 the St Dunstan's surveyor wrote to Shahriar stating that while he would be occupying the house rent free, he should know that the notional rent (which he would not be charged) was £5/19s. That letter was preceded by one from a different surveyor in 1950 reminding Shahriar that while his occupation would be rent-free, the occupant of the ground floor flat would be paying rent and £20 towards upkeep! Reading between the lines, it would seem that the surveyors were not happy about these arrangements.

The ground floor was to house another family – a Mrs Wilson and her daughter Marie who had been a secretary at St Dunstan's before retiring. But the upper two floors would provide the comfort and stability Shahriar so desperately wanted for Laal, Bahram, and the child they had only recently learned was on the way.[37] The St Dunstan's archives show that the cost of the building was £3250, and St Dunstan's were to pay £1250 for the roughly one third of the house that was not to be occupied by Shahriar and his family, and Miss MacAndrew's gift covered that part of the purchase price that was for Shahriar's benefit.

In his letter, the surveyor wrote that the house would be ready for occupation by October at the latest. It felt like a miracle. Laal and Shahriar could hardly contain their joy. Several times a week, Laal would bundle Bahram into his coat, take Shahriar by the arm, and make the trip to the building site to see how the work was progressing. They would stand there together – Laal describing the rising walls, the windows being fitted, the roof tiles laid in place.

But it was slow going. Progress stalled, then stalled again. Delays crept in, seeming to rob them of the dream that always seemed just out of reach. October came and went. Winter descended with its biting winds and grey skies, and still, there was no conclusion. It was a difficult time.

Laal, heavily pregnant, grew tired more easily now, but she carried on with stoic determination. Shahriar, ever practical, reassured her: the house would come when it came, and in the meantime, they would manage, as they had hitherto.

By February 1951, four months had passed since the scheduled completion date, the house was still not completed, and the new baby was ready to arrive. On a cold February morning – 4th February 1951 – Shahin, their daughter, was born. Laal, exhausted but proud, was sent to a convalescent home paid for by the newly established National Health Service, which had begun less than three years earlier. Bahram, now a lively, but somewhat bewildered, little boy, was placed with a foster family for the interim, while Shahriar returned to his solitary routines at Mr. Watt's boarding house on Lampton Road.

It was a trying time for all of them. Shahriar's days fell back into the rhythm they had followed before Laal's arrival – early mornings to catch the bus to work and lonely evenings in his little room. But now, with the knowledge that his family was near and waiting, there was a new sense of purpose to every step he took. He held on to the image of Laal and their children in that house, living together under one roof.

At last, in mid March 1951, the house was ready. Shahriar's footsteps quickened as he climbed the stairs for the first time. Laal excitedly guided him through each room – the too large living room, the kitchen with its gas cooker and Ascot, which delivered hot water on demand, the separate dining room and the two bedrooms upstairs and a small one down. It was not grand, but it was theirs.

St. Dunstan's, with their remarkable generosity, at that time donated £160 – equivalent to nearly £8,000 in today's money – to each member setting up home. Nonnie, ever the tireless and devoted friend, threw herself into the task of helping Laal furnish the house. Laal would travel to London from her convalescent home with baby Shahin, and together they scoured shops for the basics: crockery and cutlery, a table, chairs, beds, a cot for Shahin. By the end of March they were able to move in: the house was modestly furnished but warm and welcoming – a place where a family could truly begin to build their lives, though it has to be said that Laal subsequently and regularly complained about Nonnie's taste in furniture, grateful though she was for the enormous help that she had provided.

Nonnie and Haydn's wedding photo – summer 1952

Life at the new house settled into a comfortable, if demanding, routine. Every morning, Laal would walk Shahriar to the bus stop to catch the 657 trolley bus to his work in Brentford. In the evenings, she would meet him at the stop and walk back home with him, arms linked.

In those early months, she would take both Bahram and baby Shahin with her – bundled against the cold, with Bahram's small hand clasped tightly in hers and Shahin in a pushchair. As Shahin

Shahriar at his switchboard at Alltools

grew older and more active, however, it became harder to manage both children on the short but exhausting trip. Necessity, as always, forced a solution. Laal began tying Shahin to a table leg with a harness, giving Bahram strict instructions to watch over his little sister while she left to fetch Shahriar. It was practical, if unconventional, and undoubtedly something that would raise eyebrows today – but it worked

They lived simply in their Chiswick home, and although life was better than they had ever imagined, it must have been tough. They were not well off – objectively, they were poor. The house was cold. They had a single bar electric fire in each bedroom and a coal fire in the main room, eventually replaced by a gas fire in front of which they would stand and shiver after a bath and which also served to dry their clothes on a wooden clothes horse. And on cold winter days they would wake up to a Jack Frost display on the inside of their windows.

But Laal was a resourceful housewife. She would walk the length of Chiswick High Road just to save a penny on carrots, and she stretched Shahriar's modest wages with remarkable ingenuity, even sewing and knitting all her own and Bahram and Shahin's clothes.

They even managed to save a little each week – no small feat given their circumstances. Even taking account of inflation, with just £5/10s per week[38] it is difficult to see how they could have had sufficient to put aside – though they were extremely fortunate in not having to pay any rent. Had they had to do so, then their rent would have used up all Shahriar's wages.

Their social life, though modest, was lively. As Iran's economy grew and more people began traveling to London, the little household became a focal point for Zoroastrian visitors passing through. Laal's cooking – classic flavourful Persian dishes with mountains of rice – made their home a haven for friends and strangers alike. Guests would arrive with stories from home, and the family would sit together in their living room, sharing meals, chat, songs and memories of a faraway land. And these visitors brought gifts – Pistachios, Persian sweets and very occasionally Caviar

St Dunstan's also played a part in their social lives – once a year they were invited to the 'Officers' Reunion' held in the Savoy hotel, with accommodation provided there or in the Waldorf. And they also used to arrange annual sports days on the Sussex Downs, which

Shahriar and Laal at Dunstan's Officers' Reunion in 1961, Shahriar wearing the medals awarded him by the Shah

provided an opportunity for families to get away and meet, and was great fun for their children. And though not a social activity, it is worth recording that St Dunstan's have traditionally provided a contingent to march at the Cenotaph for the Armistice Day memorial. Shahriar for obvious reasons, was not part of the marching group – the end of neither the first nor the second World War had played any part in his life. But as, sadly, the number of veterans reduced in number as they died, the number of marchers dwindled and so he was roped in to boost numbers!

Nonnie remained an important part of their lives, though her visits became less frequent after she became engaged to Haydn. Still, she never stayed away for long, and her presence was always a joy. While at Ovingdean Shahriar had also made another friend, Uncle Ron, a fellow St. Dunstaner. Ron, whose blindness was accompanied by the

Uncle Ron and Auntie Rita with Laal, Shahriar, Bahram and Shahin in the Thornton Avenue garden – summer 1955

loss of a forearm, would visit the family in Chiswick with his wife, Auntie Rita.

It both amused and horrified the children when Uncle Ron would remove his artificial hand from his stump at the dinner table and replace it with a spoon. They stared, wide-eyed, until a stern glance from Laal reminded them of their manners.

These were not grand years, but they were relatively good ones – years of quiet triumph and simple joys. In their little home in Chiswick, Shahriar and Laal built a life together, filled with hard work and the sounds of their growing children. It was not the life they had once imagined, but it was far better than had once seemed likely.

Shahriar was a devout Zoroastrian, which he manifested largely in his day-to-day behaviour. Reference has already been made to the Zoroastrian maxim of "good thoughts, good words and good deeds" and also the insistence on telling the truth. We were never aware of any untruth that passed his lips, and his straight talking could sometimes cause offence – because like other blind people he could not of course be aware of non-verbal communications, and so might not always be aware of the impact of what he was saying. An example of this was when at a meeting of the Zoroastrian Trust Fund of Europe (the umbrella Zoroastrian body at that time in London) he opposed some proposal on the basis that the person making it had been guilty of systematic deception in Iran and was making the proposal on this occasion to line his own pockets. Shahriar won the day, but made several enemies in doing so.

Zoroastrians are also supposed to pray regularly in a language called Avestan, which is incomprehensible to all but very small number of scholars. He, like all Zoroastrians, had learned the prayers by heart and repeated them by rote every morning before going to work and evening before bed, the morning prayers sometimes followed by 10 minutes of physical jerks. He never missed a prayer, and prayed devoutly.

Laal also prayed, perhaps not as frequently or devoutly, but each day, though taking a more relaxed approach – she prayed while cooking, for example, and even while pulling weeds up in the garden

It was natural for them to teach their children the Zoroastrian prayers, which Shahriar did, orally, while walking in the park – one or other child accompanied him on a walk most evenings after work and at weekends, when Laal was not doing that – and both children learned the prayers by heart.

And so in 1959, when Shahin was nine and Bahram 11, it was decided that Laal and the children should visit Iran – Laal's first visit back to her family – and that during that trip the children were to receive their 'Sedreh Pushi', the equivalent of confirmation or initiation into the Zoroastrian religion.

Shahin and Bahram (right) with cousins Mahvash and Jamshid at their Sedreh Pushi

For reasons that have already been described, Shahriar did not wish to return to Iran. He described a combination of shame, embarrassment and desire not to be the centre of attention because of his disability. It was hard but understandable. So Laal, with the children, returned to Iran nine years after she had left, to a poignant and joyful reunion with her family. Shahriar, of course, went to St Dunstan's for the first month of their absence, taking his annual holiday from Alltools – a very different stay from those that he had had previously. No training, no lessons – just, effectively, a lonely holiday, during which he reflected on the rollercoaster of his life, and how despite his misfortune, in all other respects how fortunate he was.

It had been decided that Shirin, Shahriar's mother, would accompany Laal and the children on their return to England and she would test out whether she could make England her home. The idea was understandable. She was a widow – living alone in a remote village in Iran without any children – two of whom had died or vanished, and the third blind and living in a far off land: it was only natural for her only son to wish to bring his mother to live with him and only natural that she should wish the same. But the move was not a success.

The culture shock[39] for this woman – who had only lived outside a desert village for a short time (in Tehran) – a village to which she returned when Shahriar came to England – was immense. She found the weather impossible; she would not go outside by herself; she had nothing to do all day. The combination of all these things not only made her miserable, but made Laal extremely miserable as well. And that was coupled with Shirin's return to her behaviour as a classic caricature of a mother-in-law. She wanted to rule the roost as she had when she had lived with them back in Iran, which clashed with Laal's established routines. The situation came to a head when Laal, reaching the end of her tether, expressed her frustrations to Shahriar. It was one of the few times the children witnessed discord between their parents.

Bahram remembers Shahriar, in despair – in one of the very few moments of weakness that he witnessed – saying that he didn't know what to do, torn as he was between his loyalty to his extremely vulnerable mother, and to his wife. Shahriar told Shirin eventually that she must go, not that she especially wanted to stay. So Shirin returned to Iran – and was probably not sorry to do so. Other than being near her son, the move to England had nothing to commend it.

Family life settled back into its steady rhythm. The children, encouraged by Shahriar, did well at school. Shahriar was keen to adapt to his adopted country as far as he could. He was acutely aware that English manners and customs – the English way of life – were foreign to him and he wanted to learn. One of his chosen ways of learning about the English way of life was by listening to the Archers, which he did every day without fail. He learned about things which he was convinced were normal and expected English behaviour: for example when Bahram married, he expected his wife to call him 'dad' and Laal 'mum' – as Doris and Dan Archer's daughter-in-law did.

On our walks with Shahriar to one of the nearby parks, he would make up stories – generally featuring one or other of the Archers characters and often also, for some reason, a coal man but we do not remember the details. This may seem comical – and the fact that he even insisted that both children attend scripture lessons and, in Bahram's case chapel, may seem strange decisions for a devout Zoroastrian. He was driven by the desire for maximum integration[40], and his children have him to thank for that – something the children of many immigrant families did not and do not have.

Even before that the children were sent to Sunday School, despite what their parents knew about the inclination of Christians to proselytise (and as it happens the Christian sect that ran the Sunday schools was fundamentalist and evangelical). Nevertheless, it did no harm, other than providing the children with some slightly absurd hymns about "untold millions being still untold", which neither parents nor children properly understood. They clearly felt secure in their faith, and that their faith would win through in case of any conflict.

The desire for assimilation and the intention that the children should never miss out meant that Shahriar and Laal understood that Father Christmas would bring Christmas presents, and over time led to development of their understanding of the sort of things that Christmas presents should include. The very first Christmas that Bahram remembers (when he would have been four or five and Shahin nearly two or three), he woke up in the morning to find a Christmas stocking at the end of his bed, and in it was – a tangerine. He was slightly surprised but he was told by his parents that Father Christmas always brought a tangerine at Christmas for children who had been good.

Zoroastrians, and Iranians generally, celebrate the spring equinox – the first day of spring – as their New Year (NoRuz in Farsi). Having been told that NoRuz was the Zoroastrian New Year and the equivalent of Christmas to Christians, the children wondered whether Father Christmas would come at NoRuz? So Shahriar and Laal invented Baba Jamshid – Father Jamshid – as the bringer of presents at NoRuz, never very substantial but presents nevertheless, and accompanied by the excitement that presents entailed. They used the creation of Baba Jamshid to their advantage. The following Christmas the children woke up not only to the tangerine and perhaps a more substantial present, but also a letter from Father Christmas saying that he had met Baba Jamshid in heaven the other day, who had told him that if the children were good, he would bring them a present at NoRuz.

Being a blind father of children did not in general pose many difficulties. He helped them with their homework[41]. For example, in order to help Shahin with her geography homework he had her trace and then cut out an outline of Africa in cardboard and all the countries within it, rather like a jigsaw puzzle. And then together they would identify the countries and the capitals of those countries. He even tried, with more or less success, to teach them to read and write Farsi.[42]

He also encouraged their interests and took pleasure in their pleasures. Shahin recalls for example that when she was given a budgerigar as a NoRuz present, optimistically called "Chatter", he enjoyed teaching it to talk; and when it was allowed out of its cage and perched on his head, he encouraged it to hop onto his fingers and kiss his lips.[43]

But it was not all plain sailing. On more than one occasion when Shahin or Bahram, both of whom were lively children, had been naughty and had worked Shahriar up to a rage, he wanted to get hold of them but they took advantage of his blindness and as he approached would escape to another part of the room and eventually out of the room, leaving him frustrated and even more angry. But the moment passed and for the most part punishment was not a major issue in the family despite the usual naughtiness of children

Occasionally he was too quick for the children and they were caught. But the consequence was never other than a serious telling off, which from Shahriar was quite intimidating. He never, as far as we recall, smacked us. Unlike Laal! Laal was very easy-going and affectionate. But just occasionally when one of the children had been really naughty and she was at her wits' end, she would open the kitchen drawer, pull out the wooden spoon and give them a sharp smack on the back of the hand. That wooden spoon served many purposes, but the one remembered best was the infliction of a sharp pain and was never forgotten.

Shahriar had high aspirations for his children, and was convinced that education was the route to their success in English society. He had heard of only one school and one university in England – Eton and Oxford. And he wanted his son to go to Eton and then Oxford. Lady Fraser – wife of Lord Fraser the St Dunstan's chairman – took him in hand over schooling, and explained that Eton was impossible and probably undesirable, that getting to any public school would first require attendance at a preparatory school, and that it was almost certainly beyond his financial means. But, nevertheless with her help and his success in tests and interviews, Bahram obtained a scholarship to Akeley Wood preparatory school and then a scholarship to Wellington College[44] – chosen no doubt because of its military antecedents and connections. None of this would have been possible without Lady Fraser's help – just one of many ways in which St Dunstan's made life for Shahriar and his family so much better in England.

Because of their determination to treat their two children alike, Shahin was also offered the opportunity to attend Rodean, a well-known girls' independent school, to which she also won a scholarship. Fortunately for the family finances Laal wanted one of her children stay at home, and Shahin herself was happy to stay local. She did well, winning a place at Godolphin and Latymer, one of the country's top direct grant schools.

Shahriar's high expectations were at least partly met. Both children excelled in their secondary education, and both won entry to the University of Oxford, but that much was expected. Beyond those achievements, Shahin became a long-standing magistrate and an internationally recognised authority on Zoroastrianism among academics and practitioners, and Bahram a senior civil servant before creating what has become the country's most authoritative think tank in the field of higher education.

So, they were a source of joy and admiration, but also of upset – probably as in most families. The disappointments came in parallel. Bahram's politics were far removed from his own, and shortly after his arrival at Oxford, he received a letter from Shahriar, reproduced at Appendix 2, counselling him on his activities. In many ways, this may seem like a slightly amusing letter but it speaks a lot about Shahriar. The respectability that he craved was for his family – largely achieved for himself, but he wished it to be maintained through his children.

Inevitably with his and Laal's Iranian background and their children largely adopting Western ways, there were cultural clashes. One flashpoint was when Shahin, at the age of 15 announced that she was going to a dance organised at her school. It was a girls' school so they assumed that it was a dance for girls only. When they learned subsequently that there had been boys present and that she was planning to meet one of the boys the next week, an explosion occurred, with tears and foot stamping. Poor Shahin was in a most invidious position. All her friends had boyfriends, and as it appeared – at least to Bahram – that only pretty girls were admitted to Shahin's circle of friends, that is not surprising. But it was hard for poor Shahin to be out on a limb in this respect. The problem resolved itself by Shahin concealing her amorous activities from then on – and Shahriar was oblivious to what she was up to. Bahram posed no such problems unfortunately as he had few if any encounters with girls – despite taking dancing lessons and even at one point joining the Young Conservatives.

It should not be thought from this that Shahriar limited his children's freedoms to any unreasonable extent. On the contrary, as has already been said, he was keen for them to assimilate and so they were encouraged to join the scouts/girl guides, to go on holidays abroad, to hitchhike around Europe, to undertake any number of extramural activities, and to undertake paid holiday work. They even allowed Shahin, after taking her driving test at the age of 17, to then take a couple of friends camping, driving the family car bought after Bahram had passed his test.

Beyond such questions as Bahram and his politics and Shahin and her amours, they also harboured hopes that the children would marry into the Iranian Zoroastrian community – something perhaps that clashed with Shahriar's views about the importance of integration. There was never really any question of their doing so, but perhaps their parents lived in hope, and indeed Bahram much later found that an informal agreement had been reached that he should marry the daughter of a very wealthy, and distantly related, family now living in America. He knew nothing of this but that is probably because Laal and Shahriar knew that he would be outraged at the suggestion. On the other hand, when Iranian suitors enquired about Shahin, they were adamant that first she must finish her education before there could be any question of marriage, and then that she should decide herself whom she would marry.

In both cases, their marriages (in the case of Bahram his first marriage) ended in divorce, perhaps leaving their parents feeling vindicated about their unfulfilled hopes, but also leaving them with a problem. In Iranian, certainly in Zoroastrian, culture a divorce was highly unusual, and stained a family's reputation – not just the immediate family, but the extended family as well. And so, if it became known that the children had divorced, it would very likely harm the prospects of their cousins who had not yet married. Eventually it mattered less and there was no secret, particularly after grandchildren appeared.

The family had two holidays in Southsea in the 1950s and two in Boscombe in the 1960s, where they would stay in a typical seaside boarding house which provided breakfast and evening meals.

And on two other occasions while the parents went on holiday to the St Dunstan's residence in Ovingdean the children stayed with a lady in

Shahriar on holiday in Southsea

Bexhill Mrs Hann – who used to take in children. St Dunstan's also helped here. They would provide £6 per week per family with two children as a holiday allowance – that was the allowance stated in the 1949 members' handbook and no doubt increased subsequently. This may not have been enough even in those days to pay for a week at a boarding-house, but it would certainly have contributed substantially.

Shahriar's working life came to an end in December 1959 when the Alltools factory closed and he was made redundant – almost exactly 10 years to the day after he had started there – and the family was obliged to live on his unemployment pay[45] (albeit supplemented, we think, by some form of disability allowance, paid either by St Dunstan's or which he received as a normal state entitlement).

So, suddenly their household income collapsed: his pension from Iran was still stuck in an Iranian bank, and although increasing steadily, that was no comfort for the family in England. Life must have become harder – though the children were unaware of this. And his son was at a fee-paying school. He had to face the possibility that Bahram would have to be withdrawn from his school, and that Wellington was very likely an unaffordable prospect. So Bahram took the 11+ examination for entry into a state grammar school. He failed. He sat an exam that utterly bewildered him and which he called stupid because it consisted of IQ type tests for which he had had no preparation (though only two years earlier he had taken an IQ test as part of his preparatory school scholarship requirements and was found to have an IQ of 147). Shahriar would not countenance Bahram going to a secondary modern school and so, God knows how, they managed to keep him at Akeley Wood, drawing on the savings that they had managed to make over the years and his unemployment benefit.

Two years later, in 1962, exchange controls were relaxed in Iran. He received his accumulated pension just in time for Bahram's entry to Wellington later that year, and Shahriar was also able to buy a house in Ealing Common followed by another in Chiswick,[46] to let and bring in income. As a result the family was from then on able to live reasonably comfortably. But it was touch and go.

The St Dunstan's records show that during the 1960s, after having been made redundant by Alltools, Shahriar gave as his profession "Education Adviser". We can only assume that this was a reference to the fact that an increasing number of Iranians, and Zoroastrians among them, were sending their children to the UK for education. With increasing frequency we found as we grew older that one or more of them were coming to stay for various periods during school holidays – and indeed we know that in one or two cases Shahriar acted as formal Guardian. It could be that he supplemented his income with payments from parents for his efforts.

Shahriar was uncompromising in respect of his politics and social policy. He, for example supported the death penalty saying that if there was a weed in your garden you pulled it out, or if a dog persistently worried sheep you would put it down – we should be concerned with the health of society as a whole, not with the individual. That was, though, slightly counter to his more general views which very much supported the underdog and the unfortunate – something also manifested in the donations that Laal and Shahriar gave to charity.[47] He also brought with him from Iran some mild prejudices. He was, for example, very much against mixed marriages involving a black person, which he rationalised on the basis that generations down the line a black child might be born (biologically true) which would subject the mother of that child to suspicion of having an affair.

Virulently anti-Communist, he nevertheless, because of his own experience, detested war and fighting. So when, in 1957, a large protest march took place under the banner of the Campaign for Nuclear Disarmament (CND), and passed through Chiswick, he decided that he would join the march with Bahram guiding him, and the two marched with the thousands of other marchers from Chiswick to Hammersmith – a distance of no more than about 3 miles. This march (the Aldermaston march) re-occurred year after year, but Shahriar never joined it again. When he told his friend uncle Ron – politics unknown, but probably right leaning (he and Mabel lived in Croydon) Ron was appalled and explained to him that CND was a front organisation for communists, and was almost certainly funded by and a proxy for the Soviet Union, the very same combination that had led to his blindness.

Their domestic life and division of labour was as conventional as it could have been for the period. Shahriar was the breadwinner and spent his days at work, and Laal did the housework and looked after the children. That was not an unusual arrangement. But Laal was not just a housewife – she was also Shahriar's eyes. So, for example, all correspondence had to be read by her. If there was typing to be done,

Shahriar would dictate a draft, she would read it back, and when there was a finished version, she would dictate it while Shahriar typed.

But he also did what he could in the house, although it was difficult being blind. He always washed the dishes, for example, and mowed the lawn; and we have photos of him helping to weed the garden.

However, after being made redundant, he had more time to brood and allow his imagination and inventiveness to flourish – though that is something that he previously did anyway, as manifested by his typewriter inventions. And so,

Shahriar washing dishes

Shahriar and Laal gardening at 35 Thornton Avenue

during this time, convinced of the fact that Britain would one day be sure to be more closely attached to the rest of Europe, he urged anyone interested to invest in the Channel Tunnel Company (something which he of course had no money to do). He also conceived the idea of buying vast stretches of desert in Africa, bordering on the Mediterranean and the Atlantic, and farming melons which he believed could be grown in salt water (not entirely true, as it turns out). Again, that was a plan that he was (probably fortunately) unable to fulfil himself. He also developed an interest in geothermal energy, which he saw as consistent with his Zoroastrian beliefs, because it was non-polluting; and, fascinated by the thought of free heating for everyone, he encouraged Laal and Shahin to take a holiday in Iceland to experience it and to find out more.

Family life became more complicated in the 1960s when Laal and Shahriar agreed to look after Pari. Pari was the youngest daughter of Homayoun, Laal's younger sister, and had suffered from some kind of brain damage as a baby – the working assumption was that she had had meningitis.

Pari was quite badly handicapped, both mentally and physically. There was nothing that could be done for her in Iran, but Homayoun hoped that there might be some treatment or cure available in England. And if not a cure, then at least rehabilitation and care. The family solidarity which benefited Shahriar when he went to India meant that Shahriar and Laal did not hesitate in agreeing to take in Pari.

So at the age of two and a half Pari joined the family in Thornton Avenue. Although it did not affect Shahriar too greatly, it meant that Laal, who herself was not in the best of health and eventually developed ulcerative colitis, spent endless hours taking Pari to Great Ormond Street and other medical institutions, as well as having to provide care for this physically handicapped child at home. For a while, at the urging of Homayoun who for some reason believed that rubbing the oily remnants of burned eggshells onto her limbs would enable Pari to walk, Laal spent ages in the kitchen breaking and then burning the shells of eggs, which made a horrible smell, and of course proved to be completely useless.

Pari with Laal, Shahriar and Bahram in Boscombe – early 1960s

Eventually Pari was able to walk, talk and function to a limited extent and, as she became a teenager and as Laal's health became more problematic, Pari went to a special school as a boarder, and came to Thornton Avenue only during holidays. And finally, as an adult she lived the rest of her life in sheltered accommodation.[48]

Throughout this time Shahriar's life was punctuated by occasional visits to Moorfields for further treatment – the foreign bodies in his left eye and face would from time to time flare up and had to be dealt with. But generally he was in good health, though as he got older he began to suffer from vertigo.

Shahriar was concerned about this, and about the stairs that were involved in his present home, and he asked St Dunstan's if they would contemplate moving him to a house with fewer steps. As it happens the welfare officer, paying one of her regular visits, observed

Shahriar suffering from a bout of vertigo and, seriously alarmed, put in an urgent plea that his request for a move be considered. This concern was supported by the St Dunstan's surveyor who had also visited Shahriar at Thornton Avenue and expressed a similar concern. He also reminded the Trustees of the terms of Miss MacAndrew's original bequest, under which it would be quite appropriate to purchase a new house for Shahriar and his family. St Dunstan's agreed and before too long they bought for them a conventional two floor semi-detached house at Lillian Avenue Acton, not far from Chiswick, into which they moved in July 1981.

A letter from the St Dunstan's surveyor dated 13 October 1981 informs Shahriar that their monthly rent at Lillian Avenue would be £54. So it seems that the original arrangement whereby they would live rent free in the accommodation provided with Miss MacAndrew's bequest had been changed – probably as a quid pro quo for their agreeing to buy a different house for their occupation. That would seem to have been a perfectly reasonable decision on the part of St Dunstan's, not least because the same letter shows that the rent that was being charged was just one quarter of the assessed fair rent[49] (St Dunstan's had gone to the trouble of having the fair rent assessed by the rent officer for the area). And similarly, a letter from the surveyor later, when they moved to Oxford, shows that they paid £77.62 there, but it also shows that that was about one quarter of the market rent. It would appear that St Dunstan's subsidised the rents they charged to the tune of 75%.

Once again, they were very happy in Acton until a crisis arose. In 1985 Laal broke her ankle in three places and phlebitis followed, contracted in hospital. As part of her convalescence she went to a nursing home in Hove for three weeks, organised by St Dunstan's who negotiated a 50% reduction in the normal cost, of which they paid half. And while she was there, once again, Shahriar was housed at Ovingdean.

And the following year, there was another crisis when Shahriar attempted to bleed a radiator, but unscrewed the nut too far and it fell out, allowing boiling water to spurt out continuously. He was, of course, unable to locate the nut and called Laal who, having found it, tried to reinsert it without success but scalding herself badly in the process.

She went to hospital to have her burns treated, but when she returned, she found that Shahriar had lost his memory, had no recollection of what had happened, and for a while was not even aware of who she was. Happily, that episode passed and over the next two days things got back to normal. No doubt the incident was precipitated by his feeling of panic and helplessness, and thankfully nothing like that ever reoccurred, but it was an alarming indication of how dependent he was on Laal.

Twilight years

The 1979 Islamic revolution in Iran had a profound and depressing effect on Shahriar. In fact, depressing is the wrong word. He was angry; he was upset; he cursed the Mullas, and those whom he blamed for allowing them to depose the Shah. His reaction was perhaps not surprising, given that he believed that he owed so much to the Shah and his decision to send him for treatment to the west; but also because Zoroastrians more generally appreciated the fact that the Shah and his father had taken steps to reduce the discrimination that they faced, and more positively that they promoted the religion as something distinctly Iranian and pre-Islamic. Mention has already been made that Shahriar used to sit in his chair cursing the Western leaders who, he believed, had connived in the Shah's downfall, and that is something that he returned to again and again throughout the rest of his life.

The Islamic regime stopped his pension shortly after coming to power, and that added to his rage. He was so upset and appalled at the turn that had been taken in Iran that he wanted to have nothing more to do with the country so long as it was led by its Islamic leaders. So in order to distance himself as far as possible from the country that he loved so much he changed his name from Shahriar Bekhradnia to Shahri Beck (Shahri is the abbreviated name given to him at St Dunstan's all those years ago); and he sought – and obtained – British nationality. He could not renounce his Iranian nationality – the Iranian regime would not permit that. But with the help of St Dunstan's he obtained British nationality, as did Laal, and again with St Dunstan's help they changed their name

For the remainder of his life he used to sit in his armchair fretting about Iran. God knows what he would feel now, nearly 50 years after the revolution, with the country in the state that it is in.

Shahriar and Laal spent 10 relatively good years in Lillian Avenue, but as they grew older they found even the single staircase at Lillian Avenue increasingly problematic, especially as Shahriar's vertigo got worse. And in the meantime, in 1989, Bahram and his family (a girl and boy twins (Lizzie and Dan) together with their older sister Jo, and Bahram's wife Jean), moved to Oxford, not far from where Shahin and her son Nico lived, nearby in the Cotswolds. So they once again asked St Dunstan's if they would be willing to purchase a house for them in Oxford – and they agreed.

They were extraordinarily lucky. There are very few bungalows in Oxford, and they were more or less reconciled to living in a retirement home of some sort when a bungalow became available just 150 yards from where Bahram and his family were living. St Dunstan's pounced on this and it was theirs. They not only bought the house, but did some fairly substantial work in adapting it to Shahriar's needs – for example converting part of the large garage into a bathroom with the bidet that he had longed for, and making other alterations. They also, in line with their policies and traditional generosity, provided carpeting, curtains, kitchen equipment and some furnishing as well. Shahriar and Laal moved into the house in June 1990, and that is where they spent their remaining days.

In some ways these were the best years of their lives, largely because they saw very much more than ever before of their children but more especially their grandchildren. Dan, Lizzie and Jo's school was only 600 metres away, and they regularly dropped in on their way home, generally in the hope of being offered a titbit of some sort – and generally that hope being satisfied. And Nico went to a preschool just round the corner, and would often be dropped off with them until Shahin could collect him later in the day. The interactions between grandchildren and grandparents were wonderful to behold. Especially those with Laal, who even after 40 years in England could not speak English well. The hilarity and the misunderstandings that occurred between them were numerous, and

Shahriar's 80th birthday party

in some ways the relationships were more akin to those that they might have had in Iran within a close-knit family than might otherwise have appeared possible.

It was not just Laal who took pleasure in the grandchildren and in whom the grandchildren took pleasure. Shahriar used to sit in his chair – from which he rarely moved – and when the grandchildren went to say hello he used to hold them near him and run his fingers over their faces, telling the girls how pretty they were, and the boys how handsome.

Given the turn that his life had taken, it should not be surprising that Shahriar developed a pessimistic streak. But he generally did not display that. He generally saw the positives in life – but not always. Indeed, as he grew older he perhaps grew less optimistic. Among the advice he gave to his grand-daughters (he was full of advice to his grandchildren) was that they should never accept a flower from a stranger – because it might contain drugs and if they sniffed it they might become addicted! This pessimistic streak was demonstrated also when planning permission was granted for the development of a large brownfield site near their home in Oxford. This area had previously consisted of derelict outbuildings of a factory, and waste ground. The housing estate that was to replace all that greatly improved the environment, in addition to providing housing for several hundred people. But Shahriar was against it.

Why was he against it? To him it stood to reason. If there was to be a sudden influx of hundreds of people, then in any group of hundreds of people there were bound to be some who were undesirables, robbers, rapists, et cetera. He was against allowing more robbers and rapists into the area. Laal, on the other hand, was someone who could be relied on to always see the bright side and the silver lining. She was the most optimistic, sunniest person imaginable.

During these years, they maintained their level of activity to a certain extent. The main event of the day was always when they went out for exercise – a walk round the block, sometimes into town. And it became one of the sights of North Oxford to see this elderly couple (he in a black Crombie coat and upright – she in a fur coat and bent), shuffling along the road; and nobody could be sure whether it was he pushing her or she pulling him along.

The end came in 2004. Laal had been ill with various conditions – none apparently very serious, but sufficient to cause discomfort and pain. And then in December 2003 she was diagnosed with bladder cancer. First of all treated with medication, her condition deteriorated and she went into the Churchill Hospital for an operation at the beginning of March 2004. The surgeon reported afterwards that they aborted the operation because the cancer was so dense and widespread that there was little point in trying to excise it. She was not to live very long, but there was one happy moment, when she was able to come home from hospital for Persian New Year, on 21 March 2004. She was clearly very ill and in some pain, but, as will be seen from the photo below, radiantly happy to be with her husband and surrounded by her family.

Laal and Shahriar one and eight weeks respectively before passing away

Laal (this account has been entirely focussed on Shahriar, but see Appendix 1 for a brief synopsis of Laal, to whom Shahriar owed so much) went back into hospital that afternoon and died less than a week later, on 27 March 2004, with her children and grandchildren by her side, other than Lizzie who was at their home, sitting with her grandfather, and Nico who was in the far east on his gap year.

Meanwhile, Shahriar had been growing quieter and quieter over the weeks, and we assumed that this was because he was concerned about his wife. Lizzie was sitting with him the afternoon that Laal died, and she swears that he let out a howl of anguish at what she thinks must have been more or less the exact time of her death.

Be that as it may, Shahriar himself deteriorated rapidly from then and died just seven weeks later.

Laal went into hospital in late February, and the family – Bahram and Shahin, and their children – used to take it in turns to spend the night with Shahriar, to ensure that he was safe and looked after. From time to time, and regularly towards the end, that became somewhat fraught, as he would not sleep in his bed initially, sitting up all through the night in his armchair, just waiting for time to pass. He had a talking clock – something else provided by St Dunstan's – and he would regularly switch it on, sometimes every 10 minutes or so – to be told in a slightly eerie and disembodied electronic voice that the time was 3:15 AM, 3:25 AM, 3.35 AM. It was sad and slightly harrowing for all concerned.

In the end, just four weeks after being diagnosed with pancreatic cancer and seven weeks after Laal had died, Shahriar passed away during the morning of 12 May 2006 with Shahin and Bahram both present. Meanwhile St Dunstan's had organised a live-in carer – a Marie Curie Nurse – who eased the last moments for the children and took care of everything that followed. We were very grateful to her.

It would be fitting to think that Shahriar died of a broken heart so soon after the passing of his lifelong companion and support – the person who essentially made his life possible. But such a vanity would unfortunately fly in the face of reality. The truth is that

Shahriar had pancreatic cancer, but such was our concern with Laal that we did not notice that he was yellowing nor the other symptoms. Indeed, we did notice that his face was greyer than usual but we put that down to concern for Laal. But whatever the reason, it was fitting that they died almost together, after such an extraordinary life – a life that took Shahriar from a peasant village and an orphanage in Yazd to Oxford, where he saw his two children attend one of the world's most prestigious universities and join the English middle classes.

After their deaths it fell to the children to sort out their affairs. That proved not to be difficult. We found their bank accounts were virtually empty, but for some reason they owned £1000 worth of British telecom shares; and there was a post office account book for each of the grandchildren into which they had managed to put £2 each month out of their pensions – each grandchild found that they had a little pot of about £400. Those seemed to be Laal's and Shahriar's only assets of any sort, as over time they had disposed of what little they had to their children in order, they said, to avoid any possibility of disputes over inheritance, such as they had witnessed tearing apart other families. It appears that they had been living from week to week on their pensions – almost on thin air.

So Shahriar ended his life as he had begun it, with nothing. But in a very different place and with an inspiring story to tell – or to be told. His was a life like no other.

Appendix 1

Laal

This story has been entirely about Shahriar and his life. But there should be no doubt that an equal, and in many ways greater, recognition should be afforded to Laal, who made his life possible. He would not have been able to live the life he did other than with her – and probably not with any other woman. She was his eyes; she was his rock. She was in many ways his alter ego. If Shahriar had a happy and successful family life, it was very largely because she provided the anchor and the stability – and the support – that made this possible.

Born in Yazd to Shahbahram and Gohar who had a family of two boys and three girls, her father was a Zoroastrian Dastur (priest) and poet, and also a mathematician and astronomer[50] of some note. None of those professions brought in much by way of income, so he was also

Gohar

Shahbahram

a trader who commuted between Yazd and India, in addition to carrying out priestly duties, buying goods in India and selling them in Iran. He was well educated as might be imagined but his wife Gohar, herself the daughter of a Dastur, was illiterate and remained so through her life. But she was the kindest, most serene and gentlest of women.

They had ambitions for their children, and both their sons trained and eventually qualified as doctors; and Laal and Homayoun, the two younger daughters, were young enough to be able to benefit from the only secondary school for Zoroastrian girls in Yazd, opened in the mid-1920s, and Laal went on to become a midwife.

Laal had the most generous-spirited and accommodating disposition – something she undoubtedly acquired from her mother. She accepted her lot when Shahriar was blinded and she came to England, and made the best of a life that was far from the one she had envisaged.

Beautiful though she was, as is apparent from her photos, and, presumably, much sought-after (though we do not know how many proposals of marriage she had previously received) and at 25 years old at the upper end of the marriageable age, by all accounts the marriage between Shahriar and Laal was destined to be a good one, difficult and tragic though it proved to be initially.

Immediately, she had to cope with a difficult mother-in-law with whom she did not get on and who made her life unpleasant; she lost her first child, stillborn; her husband was blinded, and sent to England for treatment after just over two years of marriage; she became effectively a single parent (though in a highly supportive family community); and not having seen her husband for over two years she uprooted and moved to be with him in a strange country whose language she did not know and whose way of life and customs were entirely foreign to her. And moreover, she was effectively moving to live with someone whom she had once known but who was now more or less a stranger.

And yet she took all that in her stride; she lived a very marginal existence in England for the first years of her time here, but gradually accustomed herself to her new life and to the fact that she had two children who had been assimilated into a culture that was not her own.

She became Shahriar's eyes – and as a blind mind man's wife she did so much more than any wife would normally do for her husband and he grew to utterly depend on her for his day-to-day living. Among other things, she even read him books in English, though much of what she read will certainly have gone over her head

And yet throughout all this she maintained a singularly optimistic disposition – would overcome any difficulty and would laugh at any setback.

Her childhood was by no means one of poverty like Shahriar's, but her family's means were very modest, the impact of which remained with her all her life. She and Shahriar lived like church mice, yet never seemed to want for anything, and even seemed to have enough to save and to go on the occasional holiday (Shahriar rarely went away, but was very keen that Laal should do so, and she went on several overseas holidays with Shahin).

She always assumed that her grandchildren – and even her children – needed money more than she did. So, whenever one or other of them went shopping she would give them a list of things to buy for her – generally a very modest list – and would insist on repaying them even if the amount was trifling. Earlier, as has been mentioned, she would sew clothes for herself and her children, and would work out where the cheapest products were in Chiswick and would cross Chiswick to buy different ingredients at different shops. And in Oxford, although she was far less mobile, she would go to the open-air market each week, buy vegetables from the different stalls, and leave a bag with each stallholder for Shahin or Jean to pick up later.

She did not always do without. When, later in life, she had a little money to spare, she indulged herself by buying what she had always coveted – a fur coat. Her sister Homayoun, who lived in much wealthier circumstance having married into a rich family, had one and Laal longed for the same. And then having bought one she proudly wore it whenever she could, even if it was not appropriate to the occasion. Once, when three of her grandchildren were appearing in a school nativity play in the local church, she arrived just before it started dressed in her fur coat, and making her way past all the other seated parents she sat in one of the seats at the front with a reserved notice on it. When someone gently pointed out to her that she was sitting in a reserved seat, she proudly replied "Yes, I know. My grandchildren are in this play"!

Strangely, although she was highly intelligent, in the 50 years that she lived here, Laal did not become very proficient at English, perhaps because she did not have a job and so her contact with English speakers was rather limited. She did, though, make efforts to learn how the English lived – for example going to evening cookery classes at Chiswick Polytechnic, just round the corner from their house; and on Sundays she would often go to church, and came home with tales of the strange rituals of 'the Christians'.

But there were some English traditions and customs that she never really understood. On one occasion, shortly after moving to Oxford, the doorbell rang early one dark evening, which she opened and was confronted with three characters dressed in black with blackened faces and witches' hats. Scared out of her wits she slammed the door shut. It was only the next day when she recounted this to Jean that she learned about Halloween and trick or treat.

It could be that one of the reasons for Laal's difficulty in integrating was because in her heart she continued to grieve for her separation from her family back home. Unlike Shahriar who had very little by way of family in Iran, Laal's family was wide, intimate and integrated, and it must have been an enormous rupture for her to leave them all behind and come to England indefinitely (she only returned to Iran once).

However, the family were all in regular contact – every week or so a long letter would arrive from Iran, often accompanied by photos, and sometimes with a tape – somewhere along the line we acquired a Grundig tape recorder, as did her brothers and sisters. She was keen to keep them abreast of the development of our family, and every few years arranged a formal photo shoot. Three of those photos, showing the maturing of the children and the maturing of the parents, are shown below.

1951 – Shahin recently born

1963 – Bahram, 13 and Shahin,11

1967 – Bahram, 19 and Shahin, 16

Appendix 2

Shahriar's letter to Bahram, with advice about his behaviour at university

This letter, sent during Bahram's first term at University, has been transcribed in its entirety but with typing – though not spelling or grammatical – errors corrected. The purpose of doing so is because it illustrates well Shahriar's strong desire for his children's successful integration into British society, his striving for 'respectability', but also the normality of their family relationships.

35 Thornton Ave
London W4
17th Oct 1967

Dear Bahram,
Yesterday morning your letter came and heard all about your new tutors, accommodation etc. It is a bit pity that you couldn't have both of your rooms side-by-side but never mind you would get use to it. What about David? What kind of room he has got or Fred Piper?

We met Lady Fraser last Saturday at the reunion and she had spread the news of your going to Oxford to every one and almost all the people there came to congratulate us and Lady Fraser said that she one day is going to come and have tea with you and also she said that last Thursday Oct.12.th she has telephoned Sir John Mode and spoken to him about you and so on. Regarding joining one of the societies, its is entirely up to your choice but mummy and I wish you to join a society which which would increase your knowledge, would bild up your sense of obedience, loyalty, humanity, duty to your Country and to your fellow creature and not joined to the Anakist, spasifist, Communist or ay society which would encourage you to be selfish, and curruption, lawlessness, thoughtlessness. etc. To make it short build a very respectable, honourable future for yourself and for all friends and those have any connection with you. Bahram, you must get annoyed when I write these things, that is because I like every other father want best for my children and want to see them grow to a useful member of society, to be respected and honoured and looked at like human and good citizen andnot like a crook, or disobedient and lowless man do something to make us proud of you as well as yourself.

Mummy has washed your pull over and is sending it now. Yesterday Mummy went to Dr Baliki and there was no medical cards, but he gave us the attached form and told us to tell you that you fill this form and take it to your college's Doctor and the rest to them. They would know what to do. Mummy and I have decided not to go to the Iran Society dinner this year and perhaps we would go next year. We are looking forward to see you in two weeks time and hear more of your new college and adventures. Mummy sends her love and wish you all the best, and success. Mummy says don't forget to eat as much as you can find and if necessary buy them especially fruit. There is no news to write so cheerio and all the best.

Your dad,
Shahriar

Notes

Childhood

1 Each was known only by their first name and patronym

2 When locusts arrived the villagers would turn out beating drums and cymbals, pots and pans in the vain hope of warding them off.

3 "Husht" in Dari

4 "Markar" in Farsi – Parsees and Iranians often exchanged an "e" and an "a" in names.

5 A census conducted after the 1979 revolution put the number of Zoroastrians at 90,000, but that is not regarded as realistic, and may have resulted from an error, or from Bahais – a minority religion regarded as apostate by the Islamic authorities and therefore even more persecuted – declaring themselves as Zoroastrian.

6 The Dari spoken by Zoroastrians (as distinct from the Afghan language called Dari, which is a localised form of mainstream Farsi) is now considered an endangered language, and a small number of academics around the world are working to record its unusual grammatical structure and vocabulary.

7 In other ways, though, Shahriar (and we) were lucky in the choice of name. In some cases a registrar gave vent to his hostility to Zoroastrians by naming a whole village "Felfelli", which translated means "Peppery". This was not an isolated example of Zoroastrians being forced to adopt pejorative surnames – another family was named "Falahati" which translates as "Peasant".

Passage to India

8 Present day Mumbai was known at that time as Bombay.

9 One of these female cousins, by a peculiar twist of fate, ended up in the UK at the end of her life and they met up in Oxford. Before coming to the UK she had started writing to Shahriar and mentioned meeting him as a handsome young man.

Teenage years

10 A tramp, holy man or Sufi

The army years: love and marriage

11 Sarlashkar Egabal Saalaari

12 In a campaign called 'Operation Countenace'

13 Morvarid Kiamanesh, the wife of Mirza Fereydoun Kiamanesh

14 The first Zoroastrian representative in the newly formed Parliament that had been created after the 1906 uprising against the Qajar dynasty, and who had been ennobled on account of his banking activities and for paying the Qajar Shah's debts, which rescued him from indebtedness to Russia where he had been a virtual hostage because of these debts.

15 The Tripartite Treaty of 29 January 1942

Tragedy

16 Renamed Urmia following the Islamic revolution as part of the process of eliminating all reference to the Pahlavi dynasty (Reza Shah and his son Mohamed Reza)

17 Shahriar himself suffered from malaria which he had contracted while on an earlier tour of duty in Kurdistan, and which reoccurred regularly until he came to England, after which it never bothered him again.

18 The Eftikhar decoration

Arrival and admission to hospital

19 Although constructed as a military airfield, starting in 1946 Northolt Airport had been in civilian use during the construction of the nearby Heathrow Airport, and by the end of 1947 was returning to military use, though still used for diplomatic and some civilian flights.

20 Called 'Tanoor' in Farsi

21 Kindly made available to us by the Archivist at the Moorfield's Eye Hospital

St Dunstan's

22 The Shah visited the UK twice more during the 1950s, but there is no record of any further direct interaction with Shahriar.

23 Dated 28 September 1955

24 For example, when Laal and Shahriar wanted to bring to the UK a rug that was in their family, St Dunstan's arranged the import. When they wanted to arrange naturalisation for Bahram – and in due course for themselves – St Dunstan's lobbied for them. And when they wanted to arrange schooling for Bahram, they did that too, with scholarships and bursaries to offset (some of) the fee. Lady Fraser even wrote to Shahriar telling him what train to catch from Marylebone in order to be interviewed by the headmaster of Akeley Wood School, and arranged a car to meet him at the other end.

25 He recalled one of the members of staff saying to him on the day he arrived "We're here to help you rediscover your strength, Captain B,".

26 In fact, this was a skill that Shahriar never used subsequently, saying that he could never have sufficient confidence to go out on his own with just a stick. Similarly, he said that he could never put his faith in a guide dog, and so he never even contemplated having one.

27 In fact, the St Dunstan's archives show that he had begun to take English language lessons while at Moorfields, which may go some way towards explaining his rapid progress.

28 Forerunner of the Royal National Institute for the Blind

29 Mehrafsoon Firouzgar (who subsequently married as Mrs Sassanfar) was one of the very few Zoroastrians in the UK at the time and had been a good friend of Homayoun, Laal's sister, when she visited Yazd. She had been told about Shahriar's stay at Moorfields and had been asked to visit him which she made a point of doing a couple of times before her return to Iran

30 The St Dunstan's handbook lists an impressive and generous range of benefits to which its members had access. These included a Braille watch, Braille typewriter, wireless sets, free wireless licences, reimbursement of travel to employment and hospital, dog licences, children's allowances, a holiday allowance of £6 (in 1949), free holidays in Ovingdean, talking book, maternity benefit of £1 per week: the list is exceptionally, generous and seemingly endless. It also goes on to say that benefits are flexible and can be provided as needed beyond those stated in the handbook. We believe Shahriar benefited from this flexibility. The Welfare Officer's report in 1994 reported that his total weekly income was £ 266.21 of which St Dunstan's paid £174.11, implying that St Dunstan's were paying a very substantial cash benefit.

31 Shahriar never knew how much, but we have learned from the St Dunstan's archives that she donated £2,000 (roughly equivalent to £100,000 today). The agreement was that the money would be used to buy a house for Shahriar and his family to live in rent free so long as they required it, and that it would revert to St Dunstan's when they no longer did.

32 The English belief in a cup of tea as the answer to all problems, whether great of small, was something that amused Shahriar all his life

33 A factory in Brentford, West London, making machine tools, which had built air frames during the war, and was now reverting to its former product line.

34 Compared with the £7/10s (£7.50) average manual wage in 1950.

35 Unfortunately a very poor photo, taken with a Kodak Brownie box camera.

Laal's arrival

36 Which had increased to £17 by 1959

Family life

37 Laal had fallen pregnant only weeks after her arrival in England and Shahin was due in February 1951.

38 One of the St Dunstan's welfare reports recorded in the archives states explicitly that "the officer has no other income"

39 Shirin brought a snuff habit with her from Iran, and to Laal's consternation used to take snuff which gave her a slightly unpleasant odour, and which she would then snort out onto the carpet! One example of the cultural difficulties that her stay caused.

40 Such was his anxiety that his children should not miss out, that on one occasion he even crossed London with Bahram to watch West Ham play Aston Villa – a team which Bahram supported for unknown reasons. A blind man watching a football match with a small boy gave rise to some interesting – but all good natured – reactions among the fans.

41 He also tried to persuade the head teacher of her school to prevent her from taking Ancient History A-level. He was alarmed at the thought of not just one but both of his children taking what he thought was a pointless subject

42 Shahin with more success than Bahram, and to her parents' delight used to write to them in Farsi during her travels

43 He was obviously fond of animals. Many years later when Shahin had a dog, Coco, Shahriar used to remark on the fact that the dog appeared to show awareness and sensitivity towards his movements and spatial surroundings.

44 Despite the scholarships, the cost of sending Bahram to these private schools was substantial. How they managed it with the wages that Shahriar earned is a mystery, though by the time Bahram went to Wellington his pension had been released from Iran, which will have eased the burden.

45 One of the rituals that the children remember was every Friday walking with him to the Labour Exchange near the Chiswick Flyover to draw his unemployment benefit.

46 He subsequently sold the Ealing house, buying another in the same road in Chiswick

47 They gave generously and eclectically to charities, but most significantly to the Zoroastrian Trust Fund of Europe to which, among other donations, they donated £2000 in 1975, which they regularly topped up in memory of his disappeared brother Shirmard, in order to create annual events for young Zoroastrians. They also gave generously to UK charities at Christmas.

48 Pari died from deep vein thrombosis in 2001 at the age of 42.

49 The 1965 Rent Act put in place rent officers for each local authority whose job it was to assess "fair rents" for a property that was referred to them, which then became the maximum that could be charged in rent. This legislation was repealed by the Thatcher government in 1980.

Laal

50 Laal remembered him on their flat roof with his sextant and astrolabe charting the stars and planets.